PRAISE FOR *COMFORT FOR THE GRIEVING SPOUSE'S HEART*

"Gary Roe is no stranger to grief. In *Comfort for the Grieving Spouse's Heart*, he captures the silent anguish of the grieving and provides practical understanding and insight for how to deal with grief. I found myself saying, 'YES, YES, YES!' with every page. If you find yourself in the midst of grief, this is a must read to help make sense of it all."

– Dr. Troy Allen, Pastor

"The author's ability to connect with the grieving spouse's heart is so evident in this book. Readers will see themselves on almost every page and find the comfort they need in Gary's compassionate empathy and counsel. I highly recommend this book to anyone experiencing the loss of a spouse."

– Paul Casale, Licensed Professional Counselor/
Marriage and Family Therapist

"Healing from the loss of a spouse is hard work. To do it well, we need to engage the bereavement challenge every day. In *Comfort for the Grieving Spouse's Heart*, Gary guides the reader through the healing process with a daily dose of honesty, courage, compassion and love."

– Dr. Craig Borchardt, President / CEO, Hospice Brazos Valley

"In *Comfort for the Grieving Spouse's Heart*, Gary masterfully describes the tapestry of emotion experienced by those affected by the loss of a mate. His connection to the reader is demonstrated through sharing his own journey of loss and healing. I share his books with clients and friends with great confidence."

– Carrie Andree, Licensed Professional Counselor

"Gary Roe seems to have the ability to put into words exactly what my heart felt after the loss of my spouse. His writings are full of truth and healing. Thank you, Gary, for using your personal pain to help others on their grief journey."

– Page Bratcher, Grief and Divorce Recovery Coach

"An easy to read book with short, daily chapters. The format offers a unique way to deal with grief. I especially like the affirmations at the end of each chapter. Be sure to read the Summary of Grief Affirmations at the end of the book."

– Cindy Fanning, Licensed Medical Social Worker, Hospice Bereavement Coordinator

COMFORT
FOR THE *Grieving*
SPOUSE'S
HEART

HOPE AND HEALING AFTER
LOSING YOUR PARTNER

GARY ROE

Thank you for purchasing *Comfort for the Grieving Spouse's Heart*.
These pages are designed to be a companion
for you in your grief journey.
Please don't read this book just once.
Pick it up again in 6 months or a year later.
Come to it again and again.
Each time you will be at a different place.
You'll see your progress. You'll be encouraged.
And you'll find your hope has grown.

As a thanks, please accept this gift – an exclusive,
free, printable PDF for readers of this book.
Download yours today:
Healing Affirmations for Grieving Hearts
https://www.garyroe.com/healing-affirmations-for-grieving-hearts/

Comfort for the Grieving Spouse's Heart:
Hope and Healing After Losing Your Partner
Copyright © 2019 by Gary Roe All rights reserved. First Edition:

Formatting: Streetlight Graphics

ISBN: 978-1-950382-20-0

Published by: Healing Resources Publishing All Bible references are from **THE HOLY BIBLE, NEW INTERNATIONAL VERSION®, NIV® Copyright © 1973, 1978, 1984, 2011 by Biblica, Inc.® Used by permission. All rights reserved worldwide.**

OTHER BOOKS BY GARY ROE

Difference Maker:
Overcoming Adversity and Turning Pain into Purpose,
Every Day

Living on the Edge: How to Fight and Win the Battle
for Your Mind and Heart

Comfort for the Grieving Heart:
Hope and Encouragement in Times of Loss

Teen Grief: Caring for the Grieving Teenage Heart

Shattered: Surviving the Loss of a Child

Please Be Patient, I'm Grieving:
How to Care for and Support the Grieving Heart

Heartbroken: Healing from the Loss of a Spouse

Surviving the Holidays Without You:
Navigating Grief During Special Seasons

Saying Goodbye: Facing the Loss of a Loved One
(co-author)

Not Quite Healed:
40 Truths for Male Survivors of Childhood Sexual Abuse
(co-author)

TABLE OF CONTENTS

DEDICATION

To Jen.
I didn't think I would find love after loss. I was wrong.
You bring my wounded heart such comfort.
You inspire me more than you know.
I love you.

ACKNOWLEDGEMENTS

Special thanks to Kathy Trim, Anni Welborne, Brian Kenney, and Kelli Levey Reynolds for their keen proofreading eyes and editorial assistance. I appreciate you more than you know.

Thanks to Dr. Craig Borchardt of Hospice Brazos Valley for his continued support in producing quality resources for grieving hearts. It's an honor to work under your supervision.

Thanks to Glendon Haddix of Streetlight Graphics for his artistic skill and expertise in design and formatting. Your artistry continues to bring healing and hope to many.

WHAT THIS BOOK
IS ALL ABOUT

COMFORT.

We need it. Badly.

Loss is painful. Separation hurts. Oblivious to our suffering, the world around us speeds on as if nothing happened. Stunned, shocked, sad, confused, and angry, we blink in disbelief. The pain can be immense.

We long for comfort. We look for it. Grieving hearts need it to survive.

In my own grief, I have been comforted by the compassion and kindness of others. Over the decades as a missionary and pastor, and now as a hospice chaplain and grief counselor, I've had the honor of walking with thousands of grieving spouses through the valley of loss and offer what comfort I can along the way. This is how comfort works. We comfort others with the comfort we ourselves have received.

HOW TO READ THIS BOOK

This book is about comfort. The loss of a life partner is tragic, devastating, and even traumatic. My desire is to meet you where you are in your pain and walk with you there.

Comfort for the Grieving Spouse's Heart is designed to be read one chapter each day, giving you bite-sized bits of comfort over a period of time. You do not have to read it this way, of course. You may find yourself wanting to read the same chapter several days in a row, or perhaps go back and reread a chapter here and there. We all grieve differently. Read in the way that is most natural for you.

The grieving process does not follow a formula of ordered steps.

Instead, grief often comes in waves from multiple directions. We can experience various emotions and seemingly conflicting thoughts all at once. As result, I have not numbered these chapters because I don't want to give the impression that grief is an orderly and predictable process. It is more like a meandering path strewn with unforeseen obstacles.

Chapters are purposefully brief and easy-to-read. Each chapter begins with the Grieving Heart speaking, followed by some thoughts about that day's subject (shock, sadness, confusion, anger, anxiety, etc.). Each reading ends with an affirmation. I have compiled these affirmations for you at the end of the book.

WE'RE IN THIS TOGETHER

The loss of spouse can be complicated and confusing. I do not have all this figured out. I am a fellow struggler with you. We're in this together. Though grief can be terribly lonely, no one should have to walk through the valley of loss alone.

Be kind to yourself. Take your heart seriously.

Read on. May you find comfort in the pages ahead.

MY HEART IS SHAKING

FROM THE GRIEVING HEART:

I don't know where to start.

My love, my mate, my partner is gone.

I don't know what to think or how to feel. It's like I've been hit by a brick. I'm stunned. Dazed.

How did this happen? How could it? Why?

My mind is spinning. I want to scream. I open my mouth, but nothing comes.

No, this cannot be.

Where are you? Where did you go?

My heart is shaking. The world has changed.

Love is powerful. We're wired for connection and relationship. We're designed to love and be loved. No wonder the loss of a spouse is difficult to understand, let alone experience. When a mate leaves, dies, or is taken from us, our minds alternately spin and then freeze. Our hearts tremble. Our bodies can be immobilized by the shock. We're stunned. We blink and wonder what happened, how, and why. It feels as though the world has changed because it has. Our world has been altered forever. Someone we love desperately is missing.

Even if we've had other losses, this one is different. This loss affects everything. We gasp and breathe. And then we breathe again and again. Slowly. Deeply.

Affirmation: I'm stunned. Dazed. I must breathe...

YOU WERE JUST HERE

FROM THE GRIEVING HEART:

How could this happen?

*This can't be real. You're going to walk through
that door any moment, I just know it.*

The tears start to flow. They morph into sobs. I can hear myself screaming.

*Yes, I feel sick. My stomach is churning. I'm light-
headed. The room is spinning.*

Breathe. Yes, I must breathe. Somehow.

Is this what a broken heart feels like?

No, this can't be real. You were just here. I swear I can hear your voice.

I'm closing my eyes. Please be there when I open them.

Please.

It hurts – badly.

***

We're in this together. Our hearts are connected. We love passionately and deeply. When a soulmate departs, there is a tearing that occurs. The separation of two objects glued firmly together is messy, and neither object is ever the same.

Love lasts. It endures. When a life partner dies, our hearts love on. We look for them. We listen for their voice.

Then, reality hits. They're gone. We cry, sob, and even scream. The sudden intensity of grief can make us feel ill.

We grieve because we dared to love. This loss is shocking and powerful.

We let the tears flow. We let the sobs come. We scream if necessary. Our hearts are expressing our love through grief.

We will never be the same. How could we be? A tearing apart has occurred, and it hurts.

Affirmation: Because my love is deep, my grief will
be intense. Tears are natural, and healthy.

HERE COME THE TEARS, AGAIN

FROM THE GRIEVING HEART:

How could you be gone? How could you leave? Why?

My heart is shocked, stunned, and broken. Perhaps shattered is a better word. I'm in pieces, all over the place.

And I'm sad. So sad.

Then again, how could I not be sad? You're gone. I can't believe this is real. I act like you're still here. I wake up and expect to see you.

Here come the tears again. I feel like I'm crying on the inside too. Tears everywhere. I'm one giant blob of sadness.

Your absence permeates everything. Everywhere I look, you're not there. And it hurts.

I feel nauseated. Breathe. I must breathe. Breathe through the tears, through the sadness.

My heart is torn open. I'm spilling out all over everything.

This is awful.

~~~

Our heart is our most prized possession. It is the essence of who we are. When we love someone, especially a spouse, our hearts are fully engaged.

7

When a love bond like this is severed, our hearts are torn. At first, we're stunned and in shock. Then we begin to feel the pain of loss.

We shake our heads in disbelief. Our minds struggle to grasp the unthinkable reality in front of us.

Our hearts begin to bleed emotion. A cloud of sadness looms over us. We become hyper-aware of our partner's absence. Out of habit and longing, we look for them, but to no avail. The reality that they are gone smacks us again and again and again.

Loss hurts. Our hearts have been sliced open. The pain can be excruciating. The sadness can be maddeningly intense.

Yes, this is awful. Truly awful.

How could we not be sad?

We keep breathing deeply. We give ourselves permission to be sad. We let the grief come.

As our love is deep, so will our grief be.

Affirmation: I give myself permission to be
sad. I will let the grief come.

HOW COULD THIS HAPPEN?

FROM THE GRIEVING HEART:

I woke up angry today.

How dare you leave? How could you do this? I want you back. Now.

But you're not coming back, are you? No, of course not.

How could this happen? Why? I don't understand.

I'll never understand.

I don't like this anger, but sometimes it feels better than sadness. I find myself irritated with everything. My fuse is short. Frustration is bubbling just beneath the surface.

I think I'm going to explode. Maybe that would be better than holding this anger in. I don't know.

I want to scream and hit something. Maybe I should.

I'm here. You're not. I'm angry.

When a life partner dies or leaves, our hearts break. Emotions pour out and flood our being. Sadness is one of the most common feelings we experience. Anger is another.

Our mate is gone. We're stunned, shocked, and sad. We begin to feel the pain. Their absence becomes a cloud that encompasses us no matter where we go.

Questions begin to surface. How could this happen? Why? Why them? Why us? Why now? Why this way?

Satisfying answers are hard to come by. Anger begins to brew within. We feel robbed and cheated. Perhaps we feel wronged or victimized. Our hearts rail against this loss, this death. We want our love back. Now.

Love is passionate and powerful. When we feel attacked, anger is a natural result.

Anger is common when we encounter loss – especially the departure of a spouse. We love them. They're gone. Of course, we're upset. Loss has invaded and stolen our mate and confidant. The key now is expressing the anger in healthy ways.

We could do any or all of the following:
- Hit a pillow, or scream into it
- Power walk around, punching the air
- Knead some dough
- Smack a punching bag
- Write in a journal
- Exercise
- Vent to someone safe

We can't afford to let the anger smolder and fester. It will most likely leak out in less than desirable ways. We must find ways to express it as it comes.

We continue to breathe deeply. We give ourselves permission to be angry. Anger is a natural part of grief.

Affirmation: It's okay if I get angry. I will find
healthy ways to express my anger.

EVERYTHING SEEMS DIFFERENT NOW

FROM THE GRIEVING HEART:

I feel confused today.

One minute I'm sad, and the next I'm angry. I zone out and find myself staring at the walls. Everything seems strange, like I'm in some alternate reality that looks a lot like my old life. Except that you're not here.

My life is not the same at all. Everything feels different now.

Then the sadness returns. Or maybe it never left. Perhaps sadness is more like a cloud that follows me throughout the day.

My emotions are all over the place, and I'm getting less able to manage and hide them. I feel unstable. I'm not acting like myself. I feel different.

The world around me marches on like nothing happened, while I'm stuck here. It's like I've become an observer – an outsider looking in.

I miss you. Where did you go? Where did I go? I want my old life back.

What is life now? I'm confused.

When this loss hits us, our hearts crack, and emotion pours out everywhere. Some manage to hide some of their feelings, only to find them leaking out here and there in unhealthy ways. Some express their emotions freely but in such a way that is not helpful to them. Others learn ways of managing grief emotions that express who they are and their relationship with their spouse.

When this unruly combo of sadness, anger, anxiety, fear, guilt, and frustration hits, confusion naturally occurs. We've never been here before. This is uncharted territory. No matter what we thought it might be like, the terrain we find ourselves in is different than we imagined or expected. Nothing could have fully prepared us for this.

Our minds are trying to somehow make sense of what happened and this new reality that has been thrust upon us. Our hearts are reeling from the collision of life and loss. Our mate, our love, is missing. There are gaping holes in our hearts and in our routines. Some confusion is common and expected.

Learning to be patient with ourselves is important. The path is rocky, uneven, and unpredictable. Grief is more like a marathon than a sprint. Pacing ourselves along the way is more crucial than we realize.

We're not superhuman. We can breathe deeply and give ourselves permission to not have to understand all the events unfolding in our lives or be able to explain them to others. Life is anything but business as usual right now.

Affirmation: Loss is confusing. I'll be patient with myself.

FOR REFLECTION
AND/OR JOURNALING

My Grieving Heart:
*"If I were to make a list of words describing how
I've felt since losing you, I would say…"*

_____

_____

_____

_____

_____

_____

_____

_____

_____

_____

_____

_____

_____

_____

_____

_____

_____

_____

_____

_____

_____

_____

_____

_____

_____

_____

_____

_____

_____

_____

I WISH MONEY WASN'T
SUCH A BIG DEAL

FROM THE GRIEVING HEART:

I wish money wasn't such a big deal. It can be such a pain -- and so stressful.

You left and I don't know where anything is. At least, that's the way it feels. Bills keep coming. There are more expenses than I could have imagined. Losing you was enough. I don't want to have to worry about money, too.

Just having to think about finances is frustrating - even infuriating at times. There are too many decisions to make. A new decision pops up every day, if not every hour.

I miss you and want to grieve. Frankly, I could care less about money right now. And yet, I'm worried about it too.

I resent money right now. I resent all these decisions that have to be made. I resent having to talk to the bank, Social Security, insurance companies, and all the rest. Everyone wants proof of this or that. I can't get into this or that account. I need a death certificate for this, and another one for that. There's a waiting period for this. I have to wait on probate for that.

I'm drowning in paperwork and details.

I feel angry and scared. You're not here. It's just me now.

I suddenly feel nauseated.

~~~~~

Financial management can be stressful even in settled seasons of our lives. When a spouse departs, money issues quickly descend upon us from every direction. Like ocean waves, things to do and decisions that must be made keep rolling in. Our already broken hearts can feel further battered and bruised.

Bills. Phone calls. Death certificates. Banks. Social Security. Insurance. Utilities. Name changes, additions, and removals. Car titles. Real estate deeds. Investments. The list goes on and on.

We can feel violated. We're stunned and feel immobilized. We're grieving and the emotions are intense. We're missing our mates desperately. These details - which we know are important and can't be ignored - invade and nip away at us. Decisions relentlessly poke and prod our already sensitive souls. Our minds reel under the weight of a to-do list we didn't want or ask for.

Now everything falls on you. All the world is looking to you for a yes, a no, a signature, or an action of some kind. And the monetary issues you needed an answer about yesterday seem to all come with a large label that says, "Wait."

And in our digital age, finances are inevitably linked to usernames, passwords, and security questions. We understand the reasons for these measures, but they can be overwhelming at a time when intense grief is pounding our system. If we don't have a handy and easily understandable list of our financial information ready for such emergencies, these details can tip us over the edge and into feeling overwhelmed.

Though frustrating, these financial matters are part of our grief journey. Let the emotions come. Find healthy ways to express them - talking out loud, writing in a journal, sharing with others, etc. Look for some helpful, healthy people who can walk with you through this.

We grieve one step, one moment at a time.

Affirmation: Money and financial matters can be frustrating and draining. I'll handle them one at a time.

I KEEP ASKING THE
SAME QUESTIONS

FROM THE GRIEVING HEART:

I miss you. Badly.

I have one of your voicemails saved. I find myself listening to it over and over. I can't believe you're gone.

How did this happen? Why? Why you?

I keep asking the same questions. My mind runs around the same track, again and again. I feel like I'm going in circles.

And yet, I'm going nowhere. I'm barely moving at all. I go from thing to thing, person to person, without seeing anything. I'm a shadow, flitting in and out of what the rest of the world calls "normal life."

What's normal now? Nothing. Everything has changed. I don't like this world anymore because you're not in it.

Can you hear me? Where are you?

I look around. It seems like the same world, but it's not. Far from it.

I'm a ball of emotion. Sad. Angry. Frustrated. Confused. Sometimes it's hard to tell one emotion from another. I feel hijacked, like I've been kidnapped and taken to some alternate reality.

Surreal. That's the word I was looking for.

Our hearts are broken. We've taken a massive hit, and our minds are in survival mode. The unbelievable has happened. The unthinkable has taken place. No wonder we're spinning.

Our souls grapple to understand this new reality of a world without our soulmate. We will always deny what we are not prepared to accept, and we're certainly not ready to accept life without them yet. Even though they're gone, their place in our hearts remains secure. We look for them. We listen for their voice. We try to keep them close any way we can. Pictures. Videos. Texts. Voicemails. Letters. Our search is part of love in action.

Each morning we expect to wake in the same world as yesterday. After a loss, this illusion is shattered. We live in a different place now, one without our spouse. Everything seems off, strange, weird. Life is surreal.

Navigating all these emotions and changes can seem about as doable as a solo swim of the Pacific. This is no longer the same world. Not for us. We did not ask for or want this change. Loss invaded, and then grief moved in. Yes, things are surreal. No, nothing is quite as it was. Our spouses mattered. Their departure is shaking our universe.

Our minds will spin. Emotions will hijack us. Our hearts will ask repetitive questions. Our souls will search for answers. We are feeling our mate's absence.

Affirmation: Life is surreal. I'm trying to make
sense of things. This will take time.

I DON'T UNDERSTAND

FROM THE GRIEVING HEART:

Last night, I dreamed of you. We were walking through a meadow. A gentle breeze was blowing. Flowers were blooming, and there was a delightful fragrance in the air.

At first, we were side by side, and then you began walking a little ahead of me. We walked down a hill and arrived at a peaceful stream. It was so beautiful.

You walked into the water and then turned and looked at me. You smiled, and I could see the love in your eyes. Then you turned around and waded back in.

I tried to follow, but I couldn't move. I panicked. I called out to you, but you kept going. As you got closer to the other side, you began to slowly disappear. Then you were gone. I stood there, weeping. When I woke up, I could feel the tears streaming down my face.

What was that? What does it mean?

Are you telling me you're okay? Was that a goodbye of some kind? Did I just get a little glimpse of heaven?

I was glad to see you, if only in a dream. I miss you so much.

Somehow, you feel less far away today. I know you're gone. And yet, I still have you somehow.

I don't understand this at all.

It's been said that we heal while we sleep. Our bodies rest and rejuvenate. Our minds often grapple with what we can't consciously process during the day. Dreams can be an attempt to reconnect with our departed spouses and to somehow make more sense of what happened.

Not everyone has dreams of their life partner, and not every dream is a positive or reassuring one.

For most of us, our minds don't rest well after this loss. Just as our worlds are shaken, our sleep is usually affected. If dreams of our partner come, we naturally want to know what they mean. In most cases, the best place to look for an interpretation is our own hearts.

When we have dreams of our mate, it is certainly related intimately to our grief process.

Some dreams might generate more questions. Others might reassure us and bring more peace to our hearts. Still others might stir or intensify our longings.

We continue to practice breathing deeply. We will be patient with ourselves on this unpredictable journey. What we don't understand now might make more sense later. We should seriously consider what our heart is telling us and grieve as well as we know how at this point in our journey. As we learn to live one moment, one day at a time, we'll be taking giant steps in understanding our grief.

Affirmation: There are many things I won't understand. I'll be patient with myself.

I DON'T KNOW HOW
TO DO THIS

FROM THE GRIEVING HEART:

I miss you. I know I say that a lot, but it's true.

I could say, "I love you." That's still true too. It always will be.

I guess that means that I'll always miss you. I can't imagine life without you, even though that's the life I'm living now. I think it will be a long time before I stop looking for you. I keep expecting you to come around the corner, to text, or to call. I wake up and expect to feel you next to me.

I don't know how to do this. I feel terrible. I'm sad. I feel alone. Everyone's looking at me, like they're trying to size up how I'm doing. People I counted on have disappeared. I guess they don't know what to do with this either.

Why did you have to go? I know this is final, but my heart keeps trying to find a way to reverse history and make you appear. I'm not ready to let you go. I don't know if I'll ever be ready.

I love you. I miss you.

We miss them. Love runs deep in the heart. Once it takes up residence, it will not be dislodged or evicted. Love remains. Love endures all things. It knows no time limit.

Yes, we will always miss our soulmates. Love has carved a permanent place for them in our hearts and lives. Their physical presence may be gone, yet they somehow linger. Their words, actions, and influence remain, hovering around us, bouncing about in our minds. Memories have become painful and wonderful at the same time.

When loss strikes the heart, we naturally withdraw a little. Stunned, we need time to collect ourselves and begin to tussle with the unwanted and the unthinkable. When we lose a spouse, this is magnified even more. We're not ourselves at present. Our family and friends notice this and often don't know what to do with it.

We feel alone. Grief is naturally a lonely process, even if we're surrounded by people. "I'm alone in a crowd," one grieving widower said.

We miss them because we love them. We will continue loving and missing them. We might find ourselves looking for them in familiar places. Their absence will stun us again and again.

We loved, and so we grieve.

Affirmation: I'm missing you.
Feeling alone is natural when grieving.

DETAILS CONTINUE
TO STRANGLE ME

FROM THE GRIEVING HEART:

I find myself thinking about money again today. I probably ruminate on financial matters more than I realize.

I wonder what to do and who to trust. I go in circles about what decisions need to be made and what changes would be good and wise.

At the same time, there's a part of me that doesn't care. It's just money. I've lost you. That's all that matters.

Then reality settles in. I need money. I think about the future and wonder how I'm going to manage and how all of this is going to work out.

This isn't fair. You were here yesterday - at least, it seems like yesterday. Now, I live in a completely different world - alone.

I have people who care about me, but I don't have you. The emptiness is intense. The loneliness is constant. Even when I'm surrounded by people, I feel adrift, alone in a lifeboat in the middle of the ocean.

Finances are huge. And they are nothing. I despise even having to think about them. I need wisdom I don't have. I need discipline I don't have energy for. I need expertise from someone I can trust who knows what they're doing.

The details continue to strangle me. A verification call here, a death certificate needed there. Retrieve a password for this, make a phone call and get stuck on hold forever about that.

*My heart just wants all this to go away and for
you to come back. I want life as it was.*

～～～

Financial matters and money decisions can wear us down. They come at us every day. They swirl around in our minds and disturb us in the middle of the night. Perhaps we even wake panicked and terrorized. The sudden uncertainty of the future looms over us like a dark, forbidding storm cloud.

We wonder what's next. Perhaps we're internally bracing for the next disaster. Maybe some of the funds we need are tied up and on hold. Perhaps we have complicating factors such as greedy relatives and insensitive creditors. We might discover debt or obligations that we weren't even aware of.

Financial matters can set off a different sort of grief storm. If we feel left out of the loop, we can experience anger or frustration toward our departed partners. If the circumstances are stressful enough, we can even feel lied to or deceived. These things become a part of our grief process.

Whether our financial transition is fairly smooth or terribly rocky, money matters tend to stir our emotions. Our hearts want to be free to love by focusing on grieving the loss of our mates. These additional weights feel like an irreverent intrusion at a sacred time.

We might be in the equivalent of the Grief ICU - broken, bruised, semi-paralyzed, and in pain. And yet, we have all these decisions and responsibilities coming at us. Imagine a group of people crowded around a bed in an ICU unit screaming questions and waving papers (all at the same time) at a barely conscious patient. Ridiculous.

And yet, that's what it feels like to many of us.

Our hearts need space. Lots of space. The world around us screams its urgent demands. We must breathe deeply and look to our own hearts. What's most important? What can we handle next that's realistic and do-able? We'll do that, and then see.

One thing at a time. One moment at a time.

Affirmation: My heart is my most important possession. I'll
take care of it today. I'll handle what I can, as I can.

FOR REFLECTION AND/OR JOURNALING

My Grieving Heart:
"When I think about you and all that's happened, I still have questions. Like...."

_____

_____

_____

_____

_____

_____

_____

_____

_____

_____

_____

_____

_____

_____

I FEEL EMPTY

FROM THE GRIEVING HEART:

I woke up today and felt numb. I was just there. I didn't feel anything at all.

*I stared at the ceiling. I lost all sense of time. I got up
and went through the motions, hating every step.*

*I thought my heart was broken. Now I'm wondering if it
has departed altogether. I'm a shell. I feel empty.*

*I'm surrounded by your absence. Sometimes I get some relief. There are
times when I'm not thinking about you. Then something will bring you
to mind, and I feel guilty for having forgotten you, even for a moment.*

*Your absence seems to have spread and now permeates my existence.
You're not here. You're not there. You're not anywhere I'm going to be today. The rest of my life will be spent without you.*

*The thought of that is more than I can bear. I don't like
this. In fact, I hate it. I want you back. Now.*

I'm numb, but at the same time angry. Don't ask me to explain that. I can't.

I don't know much of anything right now, except that I love you.

The heart can only handle so much. Broken and even shattered, we need breaks from the constant, grinding pressure of grief and its emotions.

Our hearts shift into survival mode. Our feelers shut down. We stare at walls, ceilings, and people. We look but cease to see. Life flows on, but we are not a part of it. The sadness, anger, frustration, confusion, guilt, and anxiety all add up, and the heart powers down. We feel empty, listless, even lifeless.

The loss of a life partner changes everything.

We're numb.

We move in and out of this numb place. The heart takes a break and then begins to feel again. When the emotion gets too intense, it takes another brief hiatus. Like an electrical breaker being tripped or the emergency stop at a gas station being pushed, we momentarily switch off.

This on-and-off life is exhausting. Life is anything but "normal." In fact, nothing quite feels, looks, or even tastes the same. Grief is pounding our entire system.

We practice breathing deeply and slowly. We give ourselves permission to be emotional, confused, and numb. We take our hearts seriously. We practice being patient with ourselves. We can power down when we need to. Overall, we learn to expect less of ourselves.

Grief is squeezing our minds, hearts, and bodies. The only way to deal with grief is to grieve.

Affirmation: I may feel numb at times. That's okay. My
heart is working to manage the unmanageable.

EVERYONE WANTS ME
TO FEEL BETTER

FROM THE GRIEVING HEART:

I feel like a robot. I'm going through the motions. I don't want to go anywhere or do anything. Why can't life just stop for a while?

This is unfair. Even cruel. Everyone expects me to go on as usual, as if I'm doing great and the same person I was before you left.

Ridiculous. I'm not the same. How could I be? I'm alone now. If I just went on as before, what would that say about you and our relationship?

*You're my love, my soulmate, whether you're here or not.
I love you. I miss you. Why can't the world accept that?
Why can't my own friends and family accept that?*

Everyone wants me to feel better. No one wants me to be hurting. But how realistic is that? Expecting me to be "fine" is like expecting a head-on collision to have no effect whatsoever on the cars or people involved.

Partners aren't supposed to leave. Love is forever. Yes, we all die. Yes, I know that's natural. But it's all wrong somehow. You should be here.

I want you here.

Yes, this is ridiculous.

There is much about loss and grief which makes logical sense, but emotionally our hearts have trouble grappling with it. We're wired for relationship and built for connection. Over time, our lives become a web of relationships. When one strand is severed, our entire life-web reverberates with the shock.

Our spouse is usually the thickest, most foundational strand in our web. When that strand is broken our whole life shakes.

Much like breaking a leg, we become instantly focused on the pain and its source. What once was simple, like walking, has become excruciatingly painful and almost impossible. Routine, everyday life immediately changes into a set of Mount Everest-like challenges.

The rest of the world seems unchanged. Others' webs have not been struck, and their lives move along as usual. It feels like we've been transported to another planet and are being forced to live a different life trying to navigate unruly emotions and unrealistic expectations. And it feels like we're doing it alone.

Ridiculous. Yes, that's a good word for it.

Yes, there may be times we might feel like robots. We go through the motions, doing our best to stay functional. There is so much going on inside us, far more than we can understand, feel, or manage all at once. As much as possible, we take one moment, one step at a time. We let the grief be what it is. We try to accept ourselves as we are, in this moment.

Affirmation: I'll work on accepting myself while grieving, one moment, one step at a time.

I FEEL REJECTED

FROM THE GRIEVING HEART:

I feel rejected.

Our couple friends have changed. They were compassionate for a while, but now I sense they're avoiding me. They don't call, text, or email anymore. They don't invite me to get together or to go out.

I don't fit in anymore. I'm single now. I'm widowed. I'm not one of them.

Perhaps it's just as well. When I do see them, the grief wells up within me. I'm used to relating to couples as a couple. You're not here. You're always the elephant in the room, and we're all hyper-aware of your absence.

Uncomfortable. Weird. Lonely. Frankly, it's awful.

I've got the widowed disease and apparently, it's highly contagious. Better not get too close to me. Maybe I should wear a sign.

I'm mad. Frustrated. Confused. Hurt. I feel like everything I had has been taken from me and that I keep losing more along the way.

All our friends seem different. Maybe they're so used to us that they can't make the leap to just me.

I get that. I'm having trouble with that too.

Couples tend to have couple relationships and couple friends. When we lose a life partner, our entire relational network is upended. Perhaps the thickest, most stable strand of our life web has been severed and now all the other strands attached to it are collapsing.

This is natural, and even inevitable in many cases. But it is also frustrating, confusing, and extremely painful.

We can feel forsaken, abandoned, and rejected. If we come from a difficult, traumatic, or abusive past, our past pain can be surfaced by these current losses. We're thrust into a new world that looks that same, but where everything is different. All the rules have changed. Emotionally, we're treading water, desperately trying to stay afloat somehow.

Feeling shunned on top of the heartbreaking loss of a mate feels unfair and even cruel. The pain can strike deep and plant seeds of bitterness inside us. Our hearts can't afford this.

We must find ways to forgive quickly. We must release the unhelpful statements and actions of others as they occur. We must guard our hearts from being infiltrated by these harmful viruses.

Everything has changed. We're in pain. This will not be fixed. We've lost our mates.

Affirmation: All my relationships seem to be changing. I don't like this. I will hold things loosely, forgive quickly, and grieve as best as I know how.

I'M FORGETTING THINGS

FROM THE GRIEVING HEART:

I'm forgetting things.

Appointments. Where I put my car keys. What I came into the room for.

I'm losing words. I have trouble talking in complete sentences and making sense sometimes. I blip out in the middle of conversations, and when I come back to reality, I'm confronted by blank stares and even laughter.

I'm not myself. How could I be myself? Half of me is missing.

This is frustrating and embarrassing. It's like I'm not all here, as if part of me is fading away.

Honestly, I'm concerned, and a little frightened.

Am I okay?

I don't feel okay. I feel strange. And I feel so alone.

Some people are worried about me. Others are starting to give me this, "Come on! Get over it!" look.

Maybe they're right. Perhaps I'm damaged somehow. Maybe I'm the problem. Am I going crazy?

Losing a spouse is crazy. It hits every part of our being and our life. Grief squeezes us, and sometimes there is not much left over for living "normal" or "routine" life.

Just as our hearts have been hit, our minds are taking a beating too. Grief and the corresponding emotions are taking up more space and requiring a vast amount of focus and energy. We can find that our mental capacity may be naturally challenged and even reduced for a time.

Forgetfulness begins to show itself. Memory issues surface. We blank out, even in the middle of important conversations. We can't seem to pull up what we knew yesterday. We can't remember where we were this morning or where we're supposed to be next.

In an age when we're on the alert for mental illness, dementia, and Alzheimer's, this is scary. We naturally wonder what's happening to us. Are we going crazy?

No. We're not crazy, but we are in a crazy-making situation. We've lost someone we love dearly – our life mate. Life's usual borders are being strained. Intense and deep grief has been added to our lives on top of all that we do and are responsible for. Now there is only one of us for all this. The pressure can be immense. It can wear us down.

Yes, we will most likely notice a change in our mental capacity for a while. Our system is on overload, so it naturally eliminates items our hearts don't see as necessary to our survival.

We are not the same. Everything is affected right now, including our minds.

We're not crazy but accepting that we're not at our best is important. We can give ourselves a break. All our margin is being gobbled up by grief. This is natural and normal.

Affirmation: I feel crazy sometimes because losing you is insane.
I will learn to accept that I'm not at my mental best right now.

I'M NOT SLEEPING WELL

FROM THE GRIEVING HEART:

I'm not sleeping well.

I have trouble getting to sleep. I toss and turn. I can't seem to get comfortable. My mind races.

It's so quiet. I miss your breathing. I miss your movement. I miss you. I miss everything.

And inevitably, laying there in the dark, I find myself thinking about you. That doesn't help, but I can't drive you from my brain. I don't want to. I want to remember. I want to think about you. But I want to sleep too.

Sometimes I lay there for hours. Other nights I cry myself to sleep. If I read, that seems to help.

I wake up a lot. I have dreams that are not always pleasant. I'm looking for you even in my sleep. Some nights I wake anxious or even panicky. When morning finally arrives, I'm anything but refreshed.

I walk around in a daze. I'm tired all the time. I end up drifting off at work. I get drowsy in the car. This is not good.

What do I do with this? Do I need help? Do I need medicine?

I keep hoping this will get better, but it goes on night after night. Even if I do sleep one night, there's no guarantee about the next. I'm starting to get anxious about this, and I dread nighttime.

No, this is not good.

For restful sleep to occur, most of us need a sense of normalcy and safety. When we get smacked by a loss (especially the loss of a mate), normalcy disappears, and our personal sense of safety and well-being can be shaken. Sleep disturbances are a natural result.

Life has completely changed. Nothing is the same, including our sleep. When we lie down and the distractions fade, thoughts that we've been keeping at bay drift back into our consciousness. Our minds begin to race. We think about what happened, when, how, and why. We ask the numerous unanswerable questions and ruminate on them, over and over. We imagine what we could have done, if we had only known. Though it's time to wind down, our emotions may be gearing up.

Our partner's absence is palpable. Falling asleep becomes difficult. Staying asleep becomes a challenge. Even if we sleep, resting peacefully and waking refreshed is not the norm in grief.

It has been said that sleep deprivation is the most basic form of torture. Given the fact that grief isn't a quick journey, it's not surprising that we feel cranky, irritable, sad, anxious, or depressed. With sleep patterns altered, no wonder work performance and relationships are more of a challenge.

Letting our doctor know what's happening and what we're going through is important. There is no shame in seeking some help to get good sleep and pursue better health during this time. There are many options, both medical and natural. We should consult someone we trust. What has been helpful to others who have lost spouses? What seems to fit best with who we are and our situation? What can we do to get more of the rest that we need?

We're not crazy. Sleep disturbances in grief are common. We can be patient with ourselves and take the next step toward taking good care of ourselves during this time.

Affirmation: My life is disturbed, so it makes sense my
sleep would be too. I'll focus on grieving well
and trust this will change over time.

FOR REFLECTION AND/OR JOURNALING

My Grieving Heart:
*"If I were to list some of what's different since losing you,
I would say…"*

_____

_____

_____

_____

_____

_____

_____

_____

_____

_____

_____

_____

_____

_____

_____

_____

_____

_____

_____

_____

_____

_____

_____

_____

_____

_____

_____

_____

_____

_____

_____

_____

I TAKE ONE STEP FORWARD
AND TWO STEPS BACK

FROM THE GRIEVING HEART:

I thought I was a little better, but I guess not.

I was doing fine, having a good day, until I heard that song. It took me right back. Thoughts of you came flooding in. I was a basket case in a nanosecond.

I never know what's going to happen next. The grief is always there, slowly building up inside me. It grows until my system is full, and then along comes a person, place, aroma, word, or song that reminds me of you. A switch gets flipped. A hatch pops open, and all the pressurized emotion comes bursting out. I have no control over when, where, or how.

This is frustrating and embarrassing. I take one step forward, and then two steps back. The grief seems to be getting deeper. The more I grieve, the more the grief inside me seems to grow.

It all seems so backward. How do I know if I'm making progress? Is progress what I should even be thinking about? What does "good" grieving look like?

I find one answer, then generate two more questions. Is grief some never-ending cycle? Is there a way out of this?

I don't want to leave you behind. I can't go on with-out you — at least, I don't want to.

There must be another way.

Grief is a dynamic process. It's always moving. It's highly individual, defies prediction, and refuses to be boxed in. It's all a bit mysterious. It's a matter of the heart.

After the loss of a spouse, each day is a journey through a virtual minefield. We never know where the next grief burst is hiding. Anything can trigger it. The heart is looking for ways to express itself and to declare its love. We bump into unseen memories suddenly and without warning. Reminders of our soulmates are everywhere.

The heart is trying to find a way to live with the absence of this special person we've lost. We're thinking of and looking for them, even when we're not aware of it. Loss has invaded our lives and is demanding our attention.

One day we feel we're doing well. The next day might not be so smooth. One moment might be great, and the next we might be showering the sidewalk with tears. One minute, we're fine, and the next we're struggling to keep intense emotions in check.

Welcome to the grief roller coaster. It's full of ups, downs, and sudden twists. It yanks and jerks us here and there, leaving us gasping for breath. It's never smooth for long. And it's not over in 90 seconds either. It goes on, and on, and on.

This is not a roller coaster we chose to get on. We simply woke up one day and discovered we were passengers. What's important now is making sure our seat belts are fastened, keeping our arms and legs in the car, and riding this whirling, curling monster as well as possible.

It's hard to measure our own progress on this grief journey. There will be ups and downs, and some will be breathtaking. Some turns we will see coming, while others will take us completely by surprise. We simply grieve as best we can from moment to moment. We take life as it comes, one step at a time.

When the grief surges up and spews out, so be it. Every grief burst honors our spouses and declares our love for them.

Affirmation: I'll ride this grief roller-coaster
as best I can, one moment at a time.

WHERE DID EVERYONE GO?

FROM THE GRIEVING HEART:

This would be easier if it weren't for the people around me. At least, that's the way it feels.

Right after you left, people were everywhere. Tears. Hugs. "I'm so sorry." "I'm here for you." "Whatever you need."

Where did they all go? They disappeared. Evaporated into thin air. Poof!

No one has called, texted, or emailed. No one has made the effort to check on me. No one has mentioned your name. When I'm with people, they pretend like nothing ever happened.

But something has happened. You're gone, and you're not coming back. My heart is broken. I'm in pieces. No one notices. They just step over the rubble and continue on.

I'm not saying that no one has been helpful. Some have. I'm not saying that everyone is insensitive. Some have been kind and caring. I'm saying that most people seem to want to wish this away, and the result is that I feel invisible, crushed, and abandoned.

Losing you was more than enough. I hadn't counted on the betrayal of others.

Yeah, I'm angry.

When we lose a life partner, it affects more than we may have realized at first. Perhaps the key strand of our web has been severed and now all of

41

life is unsettled. This loss affects everything. Other strands get strained and stretched. Some might fray under the strain.

Relationships are dynamic. They never stay still. We're always growing closer or more distant, usually in small, hardly perceptible ways. When we lose a mate, all of our relationships are jostled. We head into a season of grief and pain.

Our relationships become more precious to us and we need the support and love of others during this time. Unfortunately, few people know how to care for a grieving heart. When we don't know what to do, we often end up doing nothing.

The initial loss often results in other losses. People don't come through for us, and we feel hurt, betrayed, or even abandoned. Our sense of loneliness grows, and so does our anger. Our hearts, longing to be seen, heard, and cared for, are further devastated and want to slink away into hiding.

This loss is incredibly painful, and grief is a lonely, rocky road. Finding good traveling companions can be difficult and challenging.

No one understands how we feel - even those who have lost spouses. It's *our* loss and *our* lives. It is *our* grief – uniquely ours. Other widows and widowers can empathize, but they are not in our hearts and minds. This was *our* mate, *our* marriage, *our* relationship.

When those we counted on don't even bother to show up, angry disappointment is the natural result. We must give ourselves permission to hurt over these new losses. We can find healthy ways to express the anger that comes.

Thankfully, not everyone will disappear. Others we haven't counted on will step forward. New people will surface. We might feel alone, but this grief road is well populated with fellow travelers. We aren't the only passengers on this roller-coaster.

Affirmation: Though some people might disappoint me,
I will grieve as best I can, given the circumstances.

HOW DO I RAISE KIDS ALONE?

FROM THE GRIEVING HEART:

"Now it's just me." I find myself saying that a lot.

When it comes to parenting, I feel the truth of it every moment.

No conversations with you about what to do. No backup for decisions or discipline. No help with, well, anything. And everything I do with the kids just amplifies your absence.

You were always here. Now, you're gone. None of us know what to do with that.

How do I raise kids alone?

I look ahead and see the milestones out there. Birthdays. Holidays. Proms. Graduations. Marriages. You won't be there for any of them. It will be just me. Every special day feels like it will be a knife straight to my heart.

How do I do the parenting work of two, while grieving? Frankly, I don't have time or energy to grieve. Life streaks along, dragging all of us along with it.

I feel abandoned. I feel alone. As a parent and spouse, I am alone.

It's just me now.

Parenting might be one of the most challenging things in life. We love our kids and want the best for them. Until recently, we tackled the blessings and demands of parenting together with our spouses. Now, it's just us. No parenting partner. No sounding board. No fellow decision-maker.

It all falls to us now. The sense of responsibility can be overwhelming.

In addition, we have to parent with our hearts in pieces strewn all over place. We're broken and aching, and yet more is demanded of us. We were stretched and stressed before. Now life seems impossible.

Our kids deserve our best, but we're running on fumes, exhausted and hurting. Grief is taking up a large portion of our hearts and energy. There is little to nothing left over for anything else, let alone parenting.

We need support. We need help. But where do we find it, and from whom?

In the end, we're still faced with paring life down to essentials. Self-care must be high on our list. Many things may have to go on autopilot for now.

Our families are not the same. This is traumatic and life-changing for everyone involved. We must adjust our expectations of ourselves – and others. We breathe deeply. We focus on taking care of ourselves and grieving well. Beyond that, we handle what comes at us as best we can.

Now is not forever. Without looking too far ahead, we focus on living one moment at a time, being patient with ourselves along the way.

Affirmation: Parenting feels impossible right now. I'll focus on taking care of myself and grieving in healthy ways. I'll face life one thing, one moment at a time.

WHO'S NEXT?

FROM THE GRIEVING HEART:

I miss you.

If this could happen to you, what else might happen? And to whom?

Frankly, it's terrifying. Anything could happen to anyone at any time. One minute you're here, and the next you're gone. What kind of world is this? Who's next? Is it me?

Sometimes I want to it be me. I miss you so badly. I can't see having a life without you.

I'm scared.

I want to take everyone I care about and go somewhere safe where nothing bad can ever happen. No more loss. No more departures. No more pain and grief.

I know there is good all around me, but I can't seem to see it right now. All I can think about is you. Like a rubber band, I can distance myself from grief for a little while, only to be snapped back to this unpleasant reality of life without you.

I don't like this life right now. I don't like myself. I miss my old life. I miss me. I miss you. I miss us.

We know we'll all die someday. We know all those we love will one day say goodbye and depart. Yet, we shudder to think of such things for very long. We hunker down, hoping to somehow keep death and loss at bay.

If loss hits close enough and hard enough, our stunned hearts naturally begin wondering where the next blow will fall. Who? When? Where? How? We start to sense our own mortality. Fear is often a part of grief.

Being wired for relationships, it's not surprising we try to avoid loss at all costs. We walk through life unconsciously trying to control people and circumstances to minimize any unpleasantness, hardship, and emotional pain. When loss strikes, and we realize how little control we have, our souls begin to shudder with the possibilities of what might happen next.

In times of grief, fear will likely come knocking. We can't stop the fear from coming, but if we can recognize and acknowledge it, perhaps we can keep it from busting in and making a home in our hearts.

Instead of reacting by trying to run, hide, or deny its presence, we can acknowledge the fear. "I'm afraid." We identify it, if we can. "I'm afraid I'm going to lose another loved one." Simply acknowledging and identifying the fear will help unplug its power.

Losing a spouse can be terrifying in many ways. Fear will come. It is a natural and common part of grief.

Affirmation: When fear comes, I'll try to acknowledge it, identify it, and release it.

I CAN'T GET ENOUGH AIR

FROM THE GRIEVING HEART:

I woke up afraid and panicky this morning. It was probably the result of a dream, but I don't remember one.

I'm on edge. I'm nervous and on high alert. I'm waiting for the next brick to fall out of the sky on me or someone I care about. I've noticed that my hands tremble sometimes.

I worry more. In fact, I worry about almost everything. I keep people important to me as close as possible. I'm checking on people more. I seem to be anxious most of the time.

I had an anxiety attack yesterday. I was walking along minding my own business when fear and panic descended out of nowhere. I got light-headed. My heart began to race. I couldn't get enough air. I felt like I was going to pass out.

I found a place to sit until it passed. It was terrifying. Now I know why they call them panic attacks.

What in the world is happening to me? Am I going crazy? Is this all about you and the huge hole in my heart that I can't seem to fill?

I hate this.

When we feel out of control, most of us experience anxiety. When loss invades, our capacity for handling additional stress becomes more limited. Our world has changed. Our mate is gone. Our love is missing. Our hearts are struggling to deal with all the unwanted changes that have been suddenly thrust upon us.

We're more nervous than usual. We become hypersensitive to certain things. Our baseline anxiety level rises. Over time, this anxiety can build until our systems are maxed out and can't store anymore. At some point, the dam cracks, and the pent-up emotion begins to spill out.

Anxiety is common in grief, especially after the loss of a spouse. Many have episodes of intense anxiety or panic. For those who have never experienced an anxiety attack, this can be terrifying. Panic attacks can be horrific.

Breathing becomes crucial at these times. This naturally calms the system, slowing down the mind and lowering anxiety. If we're willing to practice breathing deeply – slowly in through the nose and out through the mouth – at least once a day, we'll be far more likely to do so when anxiety or panic strikes.

Anxiety can derail our sense of well-being. Learning to breathe deeply can be a formidable skill to help us ride the grief roller-coaster better.

Affirmation: When anxiety strikes, I'll breathe
deeply and remind myself that it will pass.

FOR REFLECTION
AND/OR JOURNALING

My Grieving Heart:
*"When I think about guilt and forgiveness,
I find myself wondering about…"*

_____

_____

_____

_____

_____

_____

_____

_____

_____

_____

_____

_____

GARY ROE

50

I FEEL GUILTY

FROM THE GRIEVING HEART:

Surely, I could have done something that would have made a difference.

I laid awake last night, thinking of all I might have done or said that could have prevented this. I wanted to be able to stop you from leaving. Perhaps I can do something to bring you back?

Ridiculous, I know. Yet, my heart seems stuck there. Deep down, I believe that this is my fault. I feel guilty.

After all, someone must be responsible, right? And not knowing who that is, it might as well be me.

Is this another form of sadness? Am I mad at myself? Was I in the wrong place at the wrong time? Is this more of me trying to make sense out of what I can't seem to accept?

Strangely, sometimes the guilt feels good. I seem to need a target for this pain, even if that target is me. Otherwise, it all seems completely random and by chance, and that's simply too terrifying for my soul to contemplate right now.

I would rather feel guilty.

When tragedy happens, at first, we're stunned. When we come to our senses, we begin to wonder who's responsible for the current situation. We naturally look for someone to blame. Our anger and angst need a target. And often, the most convenient target is ourselves.

When loss attacks, guilt is usually not far behind.

Some of us are quite familiar with guilt. We grew up with it. It has been our frequent, often uncomfortable companion. Guilt moves in and unpacks its bags. It makes a home in our hearts.

Guilt is noisy. It's always speaking, filling our minds with its words and subtle accusations. Guilt's voice becomes so familiar, we begin to confuse it with our own.

Yes, it's our fault. It always is.

Guilt may be a frequent guest, but he is not our friend. His accusations and influence profit nothing. Entertaining him too much naturally leads to depression that is more than temporary. Wherever possible, it's best to recognize him, call him out, and send him packing.

Guilt is common and natural in grief. How we respond to it can make a big difference.

Affirmation: Guilt is not my friend. I must
find ways to show him the door.

THE GUILT LIST HAS NO END

FROM THE GRIEVING HEART:

I felt nauseated this morning. I don't have a stomach bug. I'm missing you.

Yes, it's that bad. Intense. Penetrating.

I've done some thinking about guilt. I'm honestly shocked at how prevalent it is. Now that I'm looking for it, I see it everywhere.

I said things I shouldn't have. I didn't say things I should have. I know I hurt you, on more than one occasion.

I could have done so much more good for you. I could have expressed my love and care more.

I could have. I should have. If only I hadn't. If only I had. I wish. What if.

The guilt list has no end. How can I make these things right? Is that possible?

I get it. Guilt is not my friend, but he is very real right now. How do I deal with this?

When a life partner departs, we naturally replay our relationship with them. We look back and review what was said and not said, done and not done. Wounds from the past surface.

Once this terrible loss strikes, our hearts are left to grapple with regrets, missed opportunities, and crushed hopes. Some plans and dreams have been shattered.

We want to take responsibility for what we did and said. We want to clear things up and make things right somehow. Our souls squirm under the pressure of unresolved issues and unfinished relational business. This is natural and common.

Many find it helpful to write a letter to their mate, expressing their love and their regrets. Asking forgiveness is important and healthy. Though we get no response, confessions like these are good for the soul. If we don't want to write it out, we can speak it. Some set up an empty chair and imagine their partner there. We can ask their forgiveness and express our love.

Forgiving ourselves can be hard. Our hearts want to hang on. For some reason, we feel that letting go of guilt means walking away and leaving our spouse behind. On the contrary, forgiving ourselves can free us to grieve and express our love more authentically.

Now is the time to begin to forgive ourselves. Our hearts will thank us.

Affirmation: I will ask forgiveness and also forgive myself, so I can be free to love you and grieve well.

PLEASE FORGIVE ME

FROM THE GRIEVING HEART:

Please forgive me. I'm so sorry.

I can almost see you sitting across from me, smiling. Are you telling me it's okay? Are you telling me I'm forgiven and to let it go?

Forgiving myself is hard. Technically speaking, it should be easy. My heart, however, doesn't seem to want to move on.

Move on? I can't believe I just said that. I don't want to move on if that means leaving you behind. They say that those who leave are never far from us. I know you're in my heart, and that's close indeed.

Is my reluctance to forgive myself an attempt to hang on to you?

Perhaps I have this backward. If I cling to guilt, I'm making it about me. I want this to be about you, and about us. Maybe I need to look in the mirror and into my own eyes and say, "I forgive you."

I know you forgive me. You would want me to forgive myself.

This is hard. Everything seems to remind me that you are gone.

Forgiving ourselves for actual and perceived wrongs is tough duty. Our hearts want to hang on, perhaps in an attempt to cling to our spouses. Forgiving ourselves feels like letting go, and that's the last thing we want to do. We don't want to move forward. We would rather back up and have life the way it used to be.

We know what was. We don't know what will be. And right now, we're stuck in the middle, in some weird state of limbo. This emotional rollercoaster is terribly taxing. Getting rid of unnecessary and unwanted baggage can be extremely helpful.

Lack of forgiveness distracts us from loving. Refusal to forgive ourselves hinders healthy grieving. Holding our own hearts captive will not bring our mates and partners back.

Perhaps looking in the mirror is a good idea. Saying, "I forgive you," to ourselves can be powerful. Some write down what they feel guilty about and then tear it up and toss it in the trash can or burn it in their fireplace. Others find an object to represent their regrets, grip it tightly, and then intentionally release it.

The key is getting the guilt out. This is part of grieving. Forgiving ourselves is an important life skill.

Affirmation: I will say to myself, "I forgive you."
This is part of loving and honoring you.

SURELY SOMEONE COULD HAVE DONE SOMETHING

FROM THE GRIEVING HEART:

Today, I'm feeling angry. Surely someone could have done something. I mean, this didn't have to happen, did it?

I wonder. Is someone responsible somehow, someone beyond me?

If I'm looking for who's potentially at fault, I don't have to look far. Yes, there are people I could be mad at. It would be easy to find a target for my anger.

I could always blame you. Why did you have to be there, then? Why did you have to do the things that got you there? How dare you leave! Did you have any idea of the devastation your departure would cause?

I'm frustrated. I want to take this out on someone and something, but who and what? In the end, I circle back around to the fact that you're gone, and nothing is going to bring you back.

I admit that the anger feels good. It feels powerful. Perhaps it causes me to feel like I'm doing something, maybe protecting you somehow. Do I want revenge? Maybe I want someone to pay.

I don't know. Maybe I don't have to know. Maybe it's enough to say, "I miss you. I'm angry that you left. I'm angry that you're not here. I'm angry you've been taken away."

I'm angry.

At some point, most grieving hearts look for someone or something to blame for what happened. Powerful emotions seem easier to express if we have a clearly defined target.

If we're looking to lay blame, finding someone to pin the loss on is easy. There are usually multiple possibilities and no shortage of candidates. Even our soulmate could wind up on the list.

Frankly, we're good at the blame game. Over the centuries we've developed it into an art form. Of course, there are times when specific people are responsible and at fault. In any case, forgiving those we perceive to be in the wrong will be key to our grief process and recovery.

Forgiveness is not saying that it doesn't hurt or that it didn't matter. Forgiveness is saying that it did hurt, it did matter, and we refuse to let what someone else did control our minds, hearts, and decision-making. We often see forgiveness as releasing the guilty party, when instead we're releasing ourselves from an invisible snare.

Our hearts can't afford to keep score. If we do, no one wins. We grow cold inside, and finally bitter. The internal rage shows itself over time, usually in self-destructive ways.

In other words, we can't afford to not forgive. Our hearts, relationships, and quality of life depend on it.

Affirmation: Blaming won't bring you back. Instead, I'll forgive.
I want my heart to be set free from unforgiveness and anger.

COUPLES SEEM TO
BE EVERYWHERE

FROM THE GRIEVING HEART:

Couples seem to be everywhere. Holding hands. Talking. Eating together. Shopping. Going to movies.

Social media doesn't help. Couples are everywhere there, too. People celebrating birthdays and anniversaries. People traveling together and enjoying life. Everyone smiling and happy. Nothing but good news everywhere.

And then there's me. Bereft. Broken. Shattered. Alone.

I'm beginning to dread going out. I see affection and connection everywhere. I feel like a kite flying alone far away from the rest of the planet. I get blown here and there by whatever breeze might come along.

I'm different from everyone else. Life goes on for all of them, while I drag along inside my personal cocoon of grief. I feel invisible, untouchable, and ugly.

I'm alone everywhere I go. At best, only half of me is left here. It was we, and now it's me. This is wrong -- all wrong.

I'm not who I was. I don't know who I am. I don't want this life. I don't like it.

No wonder seeing couples sets me off. Every twosome in the world reminds me of us.

I love you. I miss you terribly.

Seeing other couples can be painful. The grief can well up quickly and burst forth without warning.

We want the world to notice, to care. Somehow, however, we know that's an unrealistic expectation. About the only people who can even come close to truly seeing us are others who have lost spouses.

We feel different because everything has changed. Our worlds have been altered and will forever be different. We are now widowed spouses moving among a throng of couples. Every smile, hand hold, kiss, and bit of laughter are reminders of what will be no more.

We're lonely, even when surrounded by people we know care about us. Our hearts have been wounded. Our life web has been struck and damaged. We're injured and in recovery. Everything seems to remind us of our loss.

We must give our hearts their day. We must feel the grief that comes and know that each bit of pain honors our spouses and our relationships. Being in a world of couples is part of our grief process. It's not pleasant, but seeing others together gives the grief within us an opportunity to come out and be expressed.

We honor our mates by grieving in healthy ways. We breathe deeply, talk out loud, write in a journal, draw, paint, or share with others we trust and feel safe with.

Along the way, we'll meet others who have lost partners. Most of them will be compassionate, because they get it. They know. Some of them may become key traveling companions for us on this journey.

Affirmation: Seeing other couples is hard, but it is part of my grief journey. I'll find healthy ways to express the grief that comes.

FOR REFLECTION AND/OR JOURNALING

My Grieving Heart:
"Since losing you, I notice I've also lost..."

_____

_____

_____

_____

_____

_____

_____

_____

_____

_____

_____

_____

_____

_____

_____

_____

_____

_____

_____

_____

_____

_____

_____

_____

_____

_____

_____

_____

_____

_____

_____

_____

_____

_____

I'M ALL BY MYSELF NOW

FROM THE GRIEVING HEART:

I'm all by myself now.

We were a pair. A couple. Spouses. Mates. Partners in everything.

Now, it's just me.

I feel lost. I don't know what to do. I feel paralyzed. I want to take action thinking it will help, but I'm terrified of making a mistake or doing the wrong thing.

My confidence seems to have departed with you. My security is shaken. I don't feel safe. I wake up in the middle of the night terrified.

I walk around on hyper-alert. I'm waiting for the next hit. Another loss of some kind smacks me every day. Losing you is like a snowball rolling downhill.

Did you have any idea how huge you were? How much space you occupied? How much influence you had?

I guess it's true. We don't know what we've got until it's gone.

I miss talking. I miss your voice, your touch, your embrace, your kisses. I miss your smell, your presence, and your companionship. I miss you. I miss us.

I miss everything.

I must rebuild everything. My life is gone. I have to find a new one.

I don't want to. I want you.

─────◦───∿∿──

When two people become one, we become much like two pieces of paper firmly glued together. To attempt to separate them would be disaster. It's virtually impossible. Certainly, neither piece of paper would be the same. Both would be terribly torn.

That aptly describes our hearts. When two become one, going back to two again is impossible. What's left is one who is torn and full of holes.

Like two pieces glued together, we carry parts of our partner with us. Pieces of them are everywhere in our hearts and lives. They live on, in and through us. Their influence is powerful and profound. They helped make us who we are.

We carry them with us even while their absence permeates everything. Their physical presence is gone, and yet they are here - everywhere. This is why we grieve. We miss them and long for them. And yet we sense them and look for them everywhere.

We are all unique, one-of-a-kind individuals. The same is true of our spouses and our marriages. There has never been another couple exactly like us, and there never will be again. Stunningly special. Profoundly significant. Absolutely priceless.

Our grief is lonely -- and special. We're by ourselves now, but move among others who have endured a similar tragedy. We will get through this, but we will not be the same.

Affirmation: I know I need to build a new life, but I'm
not ready yet. I'm too busy missing you. For now, I'll take
things one step at a time, one moment at a time.

I HAVE MORE QUESTIONS
THAN I THOUGHT

FROM THE GRIEVING HEART:

What about God? How does he fit into all this?

Couldn't he have done something? If he is good, why doesn't he step in and prevent things like this? Why does anyone have to die?

I have more questions than I thought. Losing you has opened a Pandora's Box inside me. I don't seem to have any answers. Only questions.

And the biggest one of all is, "Why?"

Perhaps I'm angry at God. Eventually, the buck must stop somewhere with someone, right? How could he let this happen?

Maybe my idea of God is muddled. I know I'm confused right now. Not much of anything makes sense. I'm full of angst and looking for a place to unload it. I'm irritable and cranky. My fuse is incredibly short. Everything bugs me.

I feel small. Tiny. Life seems so big and overwhelming.

Sooner or later, most grieving hearts wonder how God fits into all this loss and pain. The departure of a spouse generates a boatload of questions, and the big one underneath them all seems to be "Why?"

"Why?" is often too large for us. It points to something or someone larger and more powerful than we are. After our minds trace through all the possible reasons why the unthinkable could occur, many of us find ourselves pointing an angry finger at God.

Some wonder, "Is it okay to be mad at God?" Whether it's acceptable or not, many people are angry with the one they ultimately see as having the power to prevent catastrophe and is therefore, in the end, responsible for it. No matter what our feelings are and towards whom, it's important that we're honest with ourselves about what's happening inside us.

Grief will be expressed, one way or another. The same is true about being angry with God. If possible, it's best to find healthy ways to expel our angst and frustration. Tell God about it. Speak our feelings. Write them out. Draw them.

If we have a relationship with God, it might be good to remember that the quality of any relationship is based on trust and authenticity. If he is God, he already knows what we're feeling. Be real with him. Share. Let it out. Ask the questions. Our hearts need to express what's inside.

Affirmation: When I'm angry with God, I'll be honest about it. He can handle my emotions.

I'M NOT THE SAME

FROM THE GRIEVING HEART:

Since you left, I'm not the same. I used to love going places and being with people. I loved fun as much as the next person.

All that has changed. For me, all the fun has been sucked out of the universe. Couples are everywhere. Life feels heavy. Walking through my day is like slogging through waist-deep mud.

I don't want to go anywhere. I don't want to see anyone. I want to be alone. I'm hurting, and I would prefer to hide.

Everywhere I go, I feel people looking at me. I assume they're wondering how I'm doing, or maybe what to say or do. It seems like I make everyone uncomfortable.

My heart can't handle it. If I'm alone, I don't have to worry about others, what they're thinking, what I need to do, how I'm coming across, etc. I'm not prepared for judgment or criticism, and I'm afraid that's exactly what I'm going to get.

I'm holing up here today. I'll revel in my sadness and miss you all I want. Your absence covers my world. The void you have left is massive.

I miss you.

The loss of a mate stuns us. The emotional onslaught of sadness, anger, anxiety, confusion, guilt, and frustration can be intense. Life becomes heavy. Fun disappears. Laughter seems out of place, unloving, or even irreverent.

The world looks different. Some become overly aware of the people (especially the couples) around them and what they might be thinking about us and our grief. Being in public or with others socially can become difficult. We're not on the same page as everyone else, and we feel that keenly.

For many, the safest and most logical thing to do is to go home and stay there.

When we're wounded, we naturally tend to withdraw. Instinctively, we know we need to heal. Recovery from deep, traumatic losses requires time for us to think, feel, battle internally, and adjust. And some of this is best done alone.

Yes, we need other people, but most of us also need quality time alone when grieving. This balance is unique to everyone and is as individual as every loss and each person's grief process. Time alone can be refreshing and healing. Short times of solitude remove the clamor and noise of a world that might be less than helpful to us right now.

The challenge is finding the balance of getting healthy time alone while staying connected to other people. In terms of what we need at any given moment, this balance between solitude and socializing can change in an instant. Grief is an unpredictable moving target.

Our goal is to stay flexible and pay attention to what our hearts might need from moment to moment.

Affirmation: I'll grieve well by getting the alone time I need
while staying connected to people that are helpful to me.

I DON'T KNOW HOW
TO BE SINGLE

FROM THE GRIEVING HEART:

I'm single now. I don't know how to do that.

I don't want to be single. I don't want any of this. I want you.

I see myself as married. Am I still married? It sure feels like it.

*I know this. My heart is still married. I might be widowed, but I belong
to you and you to me. Even though it's just me now, I still think it's we.*

*How can I be single and married at the same time? This is
strange. Everything seems weird, out of place, and wrong.*

*There's a huge hole in my life that's shaped exactly
like you. You're missing. Please, come back.*

*People tell me, "Don't worry. You'll find someone else." What?
Who's looking for someone else? I'm still looking for you!*

*They say, "You need to get out more." "Maybe you need
to date." "I know someone you should meet."*

Ugh.

*I wish they knew how ridiculous all of that sounds
to me. I'll never get over you. I can't.*

Single? No. My heart is still married.

To be single in our world means to be unattached. That's not us. We're very much attached. We have spouses, but they are no longer with us. Our hearts are joined. Two hearts that become one don't simply become two again.

Our hearts writhe under this dual identity that has been thrust upon us. We're married, but widowed. We're deeply attached, but suddenly single. The contradictions of our new lives can be mentally confusing and emotionally frustrating.

One thing is certain: our hearts need time to grieve, recover, heal, and adjust. How much time? As much as we need.

There are no time limits on the grief that flows from the loss of a mate. Each one of us is unique. Our marriages and partnerships were one-of-a-kind. Every spouse's grief process is their own.

Even though we're living from day to day, somehow the future is on hold. In this new world, we don't know who we are yet. We know who we were, but that has changed. So much was tied to our mates.

Grief is a process, not a checklist. We must be patient with ourselves and extremely kind to ourselves along this meandering, obstacle-laden path. We're finding our way, one step at a time.

Who knows what's down the road? We can't concern ourselves with that now. Each day has enough challenges of its own. Our task is to live from our hearts and to grieve well, one moment at a time.

Affirmation: Though I'm single now, I'm still very much attached to you. When it comes to my heart, it's still we and not merely me. I'll take my time and try to not look too far ahead.

I FEEL LIKE A SHADOW

FROM THE GRIEVING HEART:

I miss you. Your departure has stolen my appetite. I'm never hungry. I forget to eat. I'm dropping weight. When I do eat, I have to eat alone now.

When I do eat, nothing tastes good. I have no desire to eat anything healthy. Am I punishing myself somehow? Is missing you killing my taste buds?

Eating has become one more thing I don't have energy for. Preparation, cooking, and even chewing are draining. My battery is dying, and I have no idea where the charger is.

I know this isn't good, but I don't care. I don't have energy to care much about anything. I sigh a lot. I stare mindlessly into space. I drive places and then have no idea how I got there. Sometimes, I wind up someplace familiar, but not where I intended to go.

I feel like a shadow – a phantom flitting silently through everyone else's world. I function. I go through the motions. I get stuff done, but I'm not all there. Part of me is with you – thinking about and missing you. When you left, you took a piece of my heart with you – maybe even my whole heart.

Tell me this won't last forever. I know I need to eat, but my heart is starving for you.

Grief is a form of stress. As such, it tends to dull the senses. Our brains think we're under attack and shift our systems into fight-or-flight mode.

Our hearts prioritize. When in battle, food is not on the top of our necessity list.

Eating is something we used to do with our spouse. Perhaps these were times of intimate conversation and connection. Every time we eat – or try to eat – we're powerfully aware of their absence.

Grief hits the appetite. It can deaden the taste buds. Most of our energy is focused on emotional survival, and our bodies often pay the price.

We're not hungry, so we forget to eat. We're not thirsty, so we neglect to hydrate. We feel tired, even weak. Over time, our clothing gets looser. We notice changes in the mirror. We begin to lose weight.

We're usually aware of all this, but we don't have enough emotional energy to care. Apathy comes knocking, and usually gains entrance for a while. Nothing sounds good. We feel like our lives are shrinking, as if we're slowly fading away.

In most cases, this will pass with time. As we process the loss and feel the grief, our appetite will bounce back. We'll begin to taste our food again. Our energy and motivation will return.

Thankfully, now is not forever.

Affirmation: I'll try to eat well and take care of
myself. My spouse would want this.

FOR REFLECTION
AND/OR JOURNALING

My Grieving Heart:
*"If I were to catalog what's been helpful and
what hasn't in my grief process, I would say..."*

_____

_____

_____

_____

_____

_____

_____

_____

_____

_____

_____

_____

_____

_____

_____

_____

_____

_____

_____

_____

_____

_____

_____

_____

_____

_____

_____

_____

_____

_____

_____

MISSING YOU IS EXHAUSTING

FROM THE GRIEVING HEART:

I'm exhausted.

I wake up each day and sigh. My body feels heavy. Everything takes so much effort. Brushing my teeth is a workout.

Not sleeping well doesn't help. Not eating well doesn't help either. My head feels like it's stuffed with cotton. My eyes hurt.

I live in a daze. It's like I'm sleep-walking through life.

Missing you is exhausting. My heart is deflated. Part of me seems to have left with you.

What's wrong with me? I don't feel like myself at all. Who am I now? I want my old life back. I want you back.

I'm so tired I can barely think. I manage to gear up for what I must do, and somehow function enough to get through it. Then I crash on the other side. I zone out for minutes at a time.

I hope this gets better.

Grief demands incredible energy. Life in fight-or-flight mode is exhausting. Fatigue is natural and common during times of loss.

If someone was hit by a bus, we wouldn't expect them to jump up and carry on as usual. If they survived the collision, they would be transported to a hospital, preferably to one with a trauma center, for emergency lifesaving treatment. Once their life is out of danger, the stabilizing process takes time. Then the healing and recovery process can begin. During this time, all their physical energy is being channeled toward simply staying alive. Fatigue and exhaustion are routine fare for those recovering from life-threatening injuries.

We've been hit by the Grief Bus. It can stun and flatten us. We don't simply shake the collision off and walk away unscathed. Our wounds are invisible but real. The emotional pain can be intense and draining. Pain, in any form, taxes our system and exhausts us.

Rest becomes a priority. Fatigue takes a toll over time.

We simply can't do as much. Our performance at work might be off. We need more space and margin in life than ever. This is doubly difficult because, with our spouses gone, we're now most likely responsible for even more than we were. Taking ourselves and our grief seriously is critical. Being patient with ourselves is important. Like other grief challenges, the fatigue will change over time.

Our hearts, souls, and bodies will adjust and recover. Time doesn't heal all wounds, but healing does take time.

Affirmation: Grief is exhausting. I'll try to have realistic expectations of myself during this time.

I'M NOT FINE

FROM THE GRIEVING HEART:

*Wearing a mask is exhausting. No wonder I don't
want to be with people much right now.*

*I'm sad. Everyone wants me to be happy. I'm irritable, and people close to
me wonder why. Others ask how I am. Do they really want to know?*

No, I don't think they do. So, I say, "I'm fine."

*I'm not fine. And apparently, it's not okay to not be okay. People seem to
get upset because I'm grieving. I miss you. Can't they understand that?*

*I'm learning to hide. It's like I'm on stage playing a role. I thought it
might be better to keep the emotions inside when around others but
stuffing them away and trying to hide them can be totally exhausting
for me. It's like I'm having to separate from myself and my own heart.*

*I feel like a hypocrite. I don't enjoy being fake, but at the same time,
I don't want to be emoting all over everyone and everything either.*

*I'm caught, stuck, and frustrated. If I must wear a mask,
then I must also find safe places where I can take it off.*

We're wired to love and be loved, and that requires honesty and authenticity. Most of us strive to be real, but none of us are completely ourselves with everyone we meet. We're naturally more vulnerable and open with those we trust – the people we know that love and accept us for simply who we are.

In other words, all of us wear masks from time to time, depending on where we are, who we're with, and the state of our own hearts. Some masks, of course, are thicker than others.

The loss of a mate and the resulting grief pose a special challenge because the world around us typically doesn't respond well to emotional pain and suffering. We run from grief rather than drawing closer to it. We decide what's most appropriate for any given situation and we act accordingly.

Grief, however, will not be boxed that conveniently. Though we can hide it momentarily, it refuses to be silenced. The heart will express itself, one way or another.

Grieving well is not about getting rid of all our masks. It's about finding a few people we can be real and honest with — people with whom we can share our pain, frustration, and confusion. We need to feel safe. Our hearts need to be heard.

Affirmation: I will be myself and express my heart with those I trust and feel safe with. I will honor you by sharing my grief.

MY CHILDREN DON'T UNDERSTAND

FROM THE GRIEVING HEART:

My children don't understand. I guess I can't expect them to.

They keep wanting me to feel better. They keep trying to take care of me. They intervene where I don't want them to.

I feel nagged, micromanaged, and smothered. The most frustrating thing is that they don't seem to want to talk about you.

I need to talk about you. I love you. I miss you desperately. Can't they understand that I can't just pick up and move on as if you never existed?

They try to fix things that can't be fixed. I know they mean well, but I feel like they're trying to force me out of my grief and into living - whatever that is now.

I want to grieve. I need to grieve. So do they.

This is all so confusing. Your departure changed everything. Our family is different. I guess it should be. Perhaps we're all just stressed and none of us knows what to do.

Yes, that's probably it. Breathe. I need to breathe.

Our children love us and mean well. On some level, their hearts have been broken too. Like us, they don't know what to do with all this. Loss can be complicated and confusing.

We like to feel in control. As a result, we're big on taking action. We want to "do something" to feel better, move along, and somehow get out of the emotional pit that we've been thrust into.

Unfortunately - or fortunately - we're not in control. We don't control what happens next, how, or to whom. We don't control people, situations, or circumstances. About all we have control over are the thoughts we allow to take up residence in our minds and the resulting words and actions.

It's hard for children to watch their parents hurt, and vice versa. Our "fixer" genes get activated, and the temptation is to bustle around and try to make things better somehow. Deep down, however, we know there is no fixing this.

Our kids are grieving too. It would be nice if we could somehow grieve together. As parents, we can lead in this. As we grieve openly and authentically, we model for our children how to process pain and loss in healthy ways. This is a huge life skill that they will need again, and again.

Loss is hard. The loss of a spouse strikes our entire family web. Everything is altered. Being patient with ourselves and our kids becomes one of our new priorities.

We breathe deeply. We take care of ourselves and focus on grieving in healthy ways. This is the best gift we can give to our children right now.

Affirmation: I'll recognize that your departure changes all
our family relationships. This is stressful and confusing. I'll
be patient with myself and all of us in this process.

I WISH I HAD KNOWN

FROM THE GRIEVING HEART:

I've heard some things that bother me. Apparently, you didn't tell me everything.

I keep getting surprised, here and there, by things I didn't know. Things you said. Things you did.

I can't help but feel betrayed somehow. Did you lie to me? Or did you just keep things from me? If so, why?

I try to discipline my mind about this, but I can't help wondering what else I don't know. How deep did the hiding go -- and to what extent?

I'm angry about this - and deeply disappointed. I thought we shared everything. I guess in some ways that's an unrealistic expectation. No one can know anyone else's heart completely. I guess I thought I knew yours.

I need to talk to someone about this. This is eating me up inside. I have to get this out - talk it out, write it out, or something. And I know I have to let this go and forgive you. I'm just not ready to do that yet.

I never expected this to be part of my grief process.

After the loss of a life partner, sometimes the survivor hears or discovers something about their mate that they didn't know. Something they said or did. Something they didn't say or didn't do that we were under the impression that they had done or accomplished. This sets off a chain reaction of wondering.

What else might have happened? What else don't we know? What else was hidden that is waiting to be revealed?

Most of all, our trust can be challenged. When two people become one, we naturally assume that we know each other's hearts and that we share everything. This is a natural expectation, even if it's perhaps a bit unrealistic. No one knows another's heart entirely. No one shares absolutely everything.

In addition to this, not every report can be trusted either. We all have selective hearing. What someone heard our spouse say may not be necessarily what they said or what they meant.

There are times when a mate may not share something, thinking that they are protecting us. The reality, of course, is that this often backfires. Our hearts respond better to truth, even if it's scary and painful, than to discovering something later that we wish we had known.

In any case, those of us left behind get to navigate this minefield we didn't know existed. Some general grief principles apply:

Be careful what we listen to. Our hearts are wounded and vulnerable.

Find healthy ways to express what we're thinking and feeling. We must continually "get it out."

Forgive as quickly as possible - whether that means our mates, others, or ourselves.

We can also consider whether we have been totally honest with our spouses along the way. Are there things we refrained from sharing, though perhaps for good reason? If they were the ones left behind, would they discover things about us that might disturb them?

We get surprised in grief, again and again. We breathe deeply. We process what's happening inside. We guard our own hearts. We confide in safe people.

We forgive so that our hearts are not controlled by what cannot be changed.

Affirmation: If I discover something I didn't know that disturbs me, I will guard my heart. I will be honest with myself and try to process that information well.

HOW MUCH MORE AM I GOING TO LOSE?

FROM THE GRIEVING HEART:

Losing you wasn't a one-time thing. It goes on and on.

I can't watch some movies now. There are places I can't go and people that are hard for me to be with. Some foods and aromas set me off. I don't do some of what I used to, especially the things we did together. It seems like everywhere I go I get reminded of you.

I didn't only lose you, I lost most of what is connected to you — to us. Our friends. Our interests. Our favorite foods and activities. Anything that surfaces memories of you is painful right now. You touched everything in my life. It was our life.

I'm a walking ball of grief. I can almost feel it oozing out of my pores onto the ground around me. I've lost so much that it's hard to figure out who I am now.

I'm not who I was, I know that much. How much more am I going to lose?

Grief is never simply about one loss. When a spouse dies or leaves, the ripple effects begin. When this massive, central strand of our life-web is severed, the whole web reverberates with the shock. Some strands are stretched, while others might break. This one loss leads to many other losses.

The loss of a soulmate touches everything. All of life is affected. Some call this collateral damage. The result is that we not only grieve the departure of our partner but of many other things as well.

Certain places, people, events, activities, foods, smells, and music can now pack a grief punch. Anything can be an emotional trigger.

The goal is not to avoid potential triggers, but rather find healthy ways to handle such situations when they arise. Realistically, much of life may remind us of our loss, so finding ways to grieve well amid routine daily life is important.

Rather than trying to figure out what's happening – which is difficult during moments of heavy emotion – we can simply try to feel what comes and be honest with our own hearts. We let the grief come, as much as we can, given where we are and who we're around.

Our life partners touch us in so many ways. Grieving their loss is an on-going, up-and-down process.

Affirmation: I not only lost you but much of what was attached to you. I will try to be kinder to myself because this is hard.

FOR REFLECTION
AND/OR JOURNALING

My Grieving Heart:
"Since losing you, I sense my relationships
are changing. For example…"

_____

_____

_____

_____

_____

_____

_____

_____

_____

_____

_____

_____

_____

_____

GARY ROE

_____

_____

_____

_____

_____

_____

_____

_____

_____

_____

_____

_____

_____

_____

_____

_____

_____

_____

_____

_____

PEOPLE DON'T GET IT

FROM THE GRIEVING HEART:

This is hard.

Losing you was more than enough. All the additional stuff trailing along behind your departure is becoming unbearable.

I'm frustrated with people. They don't get it, and I know they can't. I don't expect them to. But a little common courtesy would be nice. If you don't have something kind and beneficial to say, well, be quiet!

Other people tell me to calm down. "They don't know what to say, but they mean well. Give them a break."

Great. What am I supposed to do? Put up with it, no matter what's said? Confront what's said and express myself? Stay away from such well-meaning but unhelpful people? Maybe stay away from people altogether?

Grieving is hard enough without feeling like I must educate everyone around me about loss and pain. I guess I think certain truths are obvious. We love. People leave. It hurts. We're never the same again. What's so hard to understand?

It's difficult being patient and kind when you feel whacked and judged.

Breathe. I must breathe.

We're made for connection, but relationships are hard. Good relationships demand attention, nurturing, and work to continue to grow and deepen. People can be difficult and unpredictable, especially when in the presence of emotional pain.

As has been mentioned before, most of what a person says is about them and what's happening inside their hearts. Most of us make almost everything about us. We're in our own skin, acutely aware of how our surroundings – including people and what they say and do – are affecting us at any given moment.

Can grieving hearts expect to be understood by the world around them? No. But it would be nice if the people in our sphere were respectful and considerate. The burden of being misunderstood and invisible, on top of the loss itself, can be crushing.

Isolating ourselves to avoid more potential pain isn't wise. We need people, connection, and interaction. We might find it helpful to come up with a few canned responses when someone says something insensitive. This allows us to respond in a planned fashion at a time when emotions may muddle our thinking.

Grieving hearts must keep breathing and take themselves seriously.

Affirmation: I can't expect others to understand my grief, but I will work to find some who will be respectful and considerate.

MISSING YOU IS
MAKING ME SICK

FROM THE GRIEVING HEART:

I miss you, and I think it's making me sick.

I can't seem to fight off colds like I used to. My stomach hurts. I get headaches from time to time. I'm always tired. My body aches.

Missing you is bad enough but feeling this way on top of it all is frustrating and confusing.

Am I sick? Is there something wrong with me physically? Do I need to go to a doctor?

I don't want to go much of anywhere, least of all to the doctor. I don't want to be poked, prodded, or stuck right now. Life is uncomfortable enough already. I don't want another person, even if it's my doctor, asking me how I'm doing, how I'm coping, or how whatever.

I don't need more questions. I need answers.

My head is full. My mind flits here and there. My heart races from time to time. My shoulders are heavy. I can't seem to get the rest I need. I'm still not eating well.

I'm a mess.

When we lose a spouse, it affects our entire system. Grief impacts us emotionally, physically, mentally, and spiritually. Many of us experience new or uncomfortable physical symptoms.

Stomach distress, headaches, aches and pains, frequent illnesses, palpitations, racing heartbeat, nausea, and dizziness are common. We can become clumsy, forgetful, and lethargic. Our bodies feel heavy. Daily life takes much more energy.

Grief is stressful. It suppresses the immune system. We get sick more often. Our bodies feel the pain of our loss and express this in a variety of ways. Weird physical symptoms often come with riding the grief rollercoaster. If something concerns us, however, it's important to get it checked out. We don't need the stress and pressure of additional unknowns right now. Grieving hearts often need support, information, and reassurance.

Our bodily distress honors our partner. We love them, and we experience their absence in multiple ways.

Rest, proper nutrition, and appropriate exercise are especially important right now.

None of us is perfect — not even close. We simply do the best we can in the situation we find ourselves in.

Affirmation: Grief is hitting my body, too. I'll be kind
to myself and take the best care of myself possible.

WHY DO PEOPLE TRY TO FIX THE UNFIXABLE?

FROM THE GRIEVING HEART:

Why do people say the things they do?

I choose to believe that they mean well, but sometimes what's said isn't helpful.

"It's okay." I've heard that a lot. No. Sorry. It's not okay. You're not here, and I'm hurting. How can that be okay?

"Don't worry. You'll get past this." Past what? Past feeling this? Past hurting and grieving?

"I know how you feel." How? You're not me. It wasn't your relationship or your loss. You don't know what's happening inside me.

Ugh. Maybe people think they need to say something. I don't know. It seems like they all want me to feel better. "Stop grieving!" is what my heart ends up hearing.

It's my heart, my life, my loss, and my grief. Why do people try to fix the unfixable?

You're gone. No one and nothing can fix that.

By nature, grief is lonely. We all experience loss, yet each person and relationship are unique. Others who have lost mates can perhaps empathize, but no one knows the intricacies of another's heart. Grief is a deeply personal and individual process.

As a result, we often feel alone. Our spouse was special. Our grief will be special as well.

Well-meaning people often end up saying unhelpful things. We can even feel evaluated, judged, and belittled by others. Grieving hearts are frequently misunderstood.

Though everyone experiences grief, we don't seem to understand it very well. We expect it to be quick – a brief rest stop on life's superhighway. We want grief to be momentary and easily resolved.

Granted, no one wants to hurt or to watch another person suffer. We would wish such emotional hardship away if we could. No wonder we fill the air with words, hoping to make a difference and bring some relief.

Unhelpful and even hurtful things will be said. For our own sake, we need to release such comments quickly and try to keep them from taking up residence in our hearts. Learning to forgive quickly is a healthy skill for grieving souls.

Affirmation: When unhelpful, insensitive words are said, I will protect my heart and release them as quickly as possible.

I FEEL VULNERABLE

FROM THE GRIEVING HEART:

Relationships are turning out to be more complicated than I thought.

I've concluded that most people don't know what to do with grief. Or maybe it's just me and the way I'm grieving.

I was accosted by a couple of advice-givers yesterday. They told me what I should be doing, how, and who with. Then they wished me well and disappeared. An emotional hit-and-run. I stood there, stunned. Then I went to my car and cried.

To top it all off, neither of these people have experienced a significant loss in their lives.

Why can't people accept where I am and simply be kind? Don't bludgeon me with words. Be with me where I am. See me. Listen to my heart.

I'm hurting. I feel vulnerable. My emotions are all over the place. I could use a few kind people who happen to be great listeners.

I need to talk about you. I miss you terribly.

Our world is full of fixers. These folks are on a mission to evaluate others and correct whatever they determine is wrong or lacking. Fixers often walk away feeling like they've done their part, while the recipient of their suggestions feels criticized, judged, or even attacked.

"You should," "You must," and "You need to..." are key phrases in their repertoire. Most fixers are far more willing to help others tackle their issues rather than deal with their own. In many cases, their attempts to fix our grief is a signal that they're trying to run from theirs.

We need people who will simply be with us, where we are, as we are. We need kind and safe people to show up, look us in the eye, and listen. It's their presence that's most valuable, not their words.

It's worth remembering that what others say to us is far more about them than about us. They're unconsciously expressing how they feel about how they perceive we're doing. If possible, limiting our exposure to fixers is important.

Affirmation: Some will try to fix me and my grief. I will remember that their words are usually more about them than about me.

I MISS YOUR VOICE

FROM THE GRIEVING HEART:

I miss your voice.

I listened to an old voicemail last night. It was wonderful and awful at the same time. I was thrilled to hear your voice, but the tears started flowing immediately.

I listened to the voicemail again. And again. I couldn't get enough of you. I closed my eyes and could almost see you. I kept them closed for a long time, my imagination basking in your presence.

Yes, I miss your voice. I miss you. I miss everything.

Since then, I've listened differently. I'm paying attention to the voices around me. I'm more present somehow. Our voices have such power. They come from within and are so personal and individual.

I miss your words, your laughter, and your singing. I listened to your voicemail again. Pain and longing speared my heart. I felt like a thousand needles had been thrust into my soul.

I'm not doing well today. All I can think about is you.

───◆───

The human voice has great power. We use it to express our minds, hearts, love, and angst. Our voice identifies us. When we hear the voice of someone we love, we smile.

When a life partner dies or departs, we miss hearing their voice. We miss the interaction and connection. We miss the physical presence and everything else associated with that voice. We remember past words, phrases, and conversations.

If we're fortunate, we have voicemails, recordings, or videos of our mate. We listen, and their voice triggers all the emotions churning deep within us. For a moment, we're with them again. Perhaps we can even somehow feel their presence.

With their voice, they spoke to us. They shared themselves with us. They told us they cared about and loved us. Their words filtered into our hearts and souls. Their voice became a part of us.

Right now, listening to their voice might bring pain and sadness. There will come a day when hearing the same message or video will bring laughter and joy. For now, we simply let the grief come. Our tears and sadness honor them. Our grief is one way we say, "I love you."

Affirmation: I miss you and long to hear your voice. I love you.

FOR REFLECTION AND/OR JOURNALING

My Grieving Heart:
"Losing you may be affecting my body and my physical health. For example, I notice that..."

_____

_____

_____

_____

_____

_____

_____

_____

_____

_____

_____

_____

_____

_____

_____

_____

_____

_____

_____

_____

_____

_____

_____

_____

_____

_____

_____

_____

_____

_____

_____

_____

_____

FOR REFLECTION
AND/OR JOURNALING

My Grieving Heart:
"Losing you may be affecting my body and my physical health. For example, I notice that..."

_____

_____

_____

_____

_____

_____

_____

_____

_____

_____

_____

_____

_____

GARY ROE

I MISS YOUR EMBRACE

FROM THE GRIEVING HEART:

*Nights are the hardest. I lay there, remember-
ing. I can almost feel you beside me.*

I reach over. My hand is greeted by the cold, empty sheet.

*The tears flow almost every night. I want to touch you. I
want to be touched by you. I miss your embrace.*

Sometimes I think, "I want one more kiss. Just one…"

*I know that would never satisfy. I keep wanting one more conversa-
tion, but I know that would only leave me wanting more.*

*I miss our intimacy. I miss lying next to you. I miss soak-
ing in your presence and listening to your breathing.*

*Our bedroom has become the loneliest place in the world. It's so
cold and empty now. And yet, reminders of you are everywhere.*

How strange life is now.

As spouses, we experience deep companionship and intimacy together. When we join ourselves fully with another individual, the intimacy involves our whole person - mind, body, soul, and spirit.

The intimacy we experience alone, just between the two of us, is priceless. This too is unique in human history. There has never been another relationship exactly like it before and there never will be again. Special. Significant.

Intimacy. Deep, soul-connected intimacy. We long for this. When we have it, our hearts delight and our lives seem to be full. When we lose it, our souls ache. We don't feel fully ourselves, or perhaps even fully alive.

For a bereaved spouse, the bedroom can be one of the most challenging places on earth.

During this time of intense grief, some seek solace in the arms of another. Though this might provide some momentary relief, the grief and loneliness will return almost instantly -- and with a vengeance. Guilt and feelings of unfaithfulness plummet down on us. We've suddenly added to our pain.

Grief must be processed well before we can find companionship that's healthy for us. If we act too soon, this new relationship may well be about us trying to replace what we had rather than about the two people involved. This isn't fair to us or the other person.

We keep breathing deeply. We take our time. We continue to take our hearts seriously. Now is not the time to give in to impulses that are potentially life-altering.

We will grieve. We will heal. We will recover and adjust. If we pay attention, our hearts will let us know if and when we're ready for a new relationship.

Affirmation: As long as I'm grieving, I'll be careful about engaging in a new relationship. I want to take my heart seriously and honor you with how I live.

MY SOUL IS LEAKING

FROM THE GRIEVING HEART:

Your birthday is coming up. What do I do with that?

I want to remember you somehow, but I'm honestly dreading the pain that I know will come.

I must bear the pain. I love you. I will remember and find ways to grieve well.

I'm glad you were born. Out of all the times and places where you could have been born and lived, somehow your life intersected mine. Amazing. Wonderful. Special.

Why did you have to go? The pain of all this grief is intense. No matter what I would have imagined, it has been worse. I guess it takes a death to appreciate what life truly means.

Did I take you for granted? I'm sure I did. I feel guilty about that. Now my heart is cracked and broken, and my soul is leaking out.

I will face your birthday and express my love for you. I will remember and honor you.

***

Birthdays used to be times of celebration. Once a spouse departs, their birthday becomes a massive grief trigger. We remember, and memories can be painful. We look at the calendar with dread, wondering how we're going to make it through this special day.

Some hunker down, close the blinds, turn off the lights, and hibernate. Others take time to remember and whisper words of thanks or gratitude. Still others make specific plans to honor their mate on their birthday. These plans can include presents, letters, cards, a special event, a donation, or serving in their loved one's name in a cause that was important to them. Some light a candle or set up an empty chair in remembrance. Many share this special occasion on social media and invite others to express memories.

Most likely, this special day will be difficult for us. It will be emotional. We might have painful or even disturbing memories. All this is a natural part of the grief process.

Our spouse's birthday will come and keep coming every year. We will fare better if we can make a simple plan for the day. Just the act of being proactive can unplug some of our dread. We can honor them, grieve well, and make the day count.

This is part of loving them, even after they're gone.

Affirmation: I will be proactive and make a simple plan for
your birthday. I will honor you and express my love.

I FEEL TRAPPED SOMETIMES

FROM THE GRIEVING HEART:

I was doing fine yesterday. At least I thought I was.

I was driving along, not paying much attention. I found myself stopped at a red light and looked to the right. There was our favorite restaurant. I lost it.

I had to pull over into the closest parking lot. I sat there and sobbed. Someone knocked on my window and asked if I was alright. I felt like a fool.

My grief is like that. It can make a fool out of me without warning. No way to prepare for it. No way to anticipate it. Every moment, I'm at the mercy of my surroundings and my emotions.

I wiped my face, started the car, and drove off. I had to pull over three more times before I got home. I sat in the driveway for what felt like an hour. I was in shock again. Stunned and paralyzed.

I go around and around in a circle. The same emotions cycle back, again and again. I feel trapped sometimes.

Perhaps this is all just my heart looking for you. I don't know. It's confusing and sad. It hurts.

As we quickly discover, grief bursts can descend upon us anytime, anywhere. Anything can trigger a memory and release the thoughts and feelings associated with it. These sudden grief spikes can feel like an invasion, an assault on our peace of mind and heart.

Though grief bursts can seem random and unpredictable, we can be proactive in how we deal with them. First, we need to accept that these bursts of emotion will come. They are natural, common, and inevitable. They can vary greatly in length and intensity. The grief is within us, and it slowly builds up over time. Along comes a trigger, and a sudden pressure release occurs.

Again, this is a natural, common, and healthy process. When a grief burst comes, we can acknowledge the emotion we feel. We give ourselves permission to grieve. If we're unable to express our grief at that moment, we can make a simple plan for when and where we will. Many times, it can simply mean excusing ourselves and heading somewhere close by that's more private.

We loved, and so we grieve. Our grief bursts honor our soulmates. By planning ahead, we can learn to handle them with increased confidence and peace.

Our hearts are expressing themselves. We're grieving.

Affirmation: I will be proactive and plan for how
I will handle the grief bursts that come.

CAN'T THEY SEE I'M HURTING?

FROM THE GRIEVING HEART:

My heart is already broken. Why do the people around me have to crush and shatter what's left of it? Can't they see I'm hurting? Don't they care?

"Life goes on, and you need to move on." I have heard this lovely, encouraging sentiment more times and in more ways than I can count. It's a knife to my soul, a blow to my gut, every time.

Yes, life goes on. Of course. But my world has changed. You're not in it, and that affects everything. My life feels like it's on pause, while everyone else appears to be speeding along unaffected.

Time is moving on, yes. But I'm not sure I am. And if moving on means leaving you behind, forget it.

I know I need to say goodbye. I've said goodbye to you many times already. Something deep inside me screams and aches. I miss you. I would rather say hello.

Though you're gone, I know that you're always with me. I carry you in my heart. Life goes on, and I am learning to go on without your physical presence.

But I don't like it. Not one bit.

Yes, well-meaning people can say some unhelpful and insensitive things. Perhaps there are times when what's said is even calculated to hurt. People get frustrated with our grief because it reminds them of their losses. Rather than dealing with their own pain and fears, they shove them back down inside and dole out curt advice to us instead.

Life moves on. Life is always moving. Time marches forward. But when we lose a spouse, our hearts are stunned and even paralyzed for a time. For all practical purposes, time stops for us. Our world abruptly halts. We move in a daze. We go through the motions, doing what needs to be done, but our hearts and souls are elsewhere.

Grief is necessary. It is a natural and normal response to a loss. It is nature's way of healing a shattered soul. We live in a new world now, without the physical presence of someone special. Their absence hovers over us and colors everything. Recovery, whatever that means for each of us, takes time.

As we walk this unpredictable, rocky road of grief, we remember our mates and find ways to honor them. We discover, one step at a time, how to take them with us as we walk life's new, yet untraveled pathways. We say goodbye in some ways, but we never leave them behind.

And we never forget. We can't. We love them.

Affirmation: I will engage in life today as best as I can, remembering you.

FOR REFLECTION
AND/OR JOURNALING

My Grieving Heart:
"When sudden grief bursts come, I can deal with them by..."

_____

_____

_____

_____

_____

_____

_____

_____

_____

_____

_____

_____

_____

_____

_____

_____

_____

_____

_____

_____

_____

_____

_____

_____

_____

_____

_____

_____

_____

_____

_____

WHERE HAVE ALL THE LISTENERS GONE?

FROM THE GRIEVING HEART:

I can't do this alone. I don't want to do this alone. Yet, I feel so lonely.

No one seems to understand. I guess that's reasonable. No one can see inside my heart, read my mind, or feel my emotions. But I want someone to understand. I need to be seen, heard, and understood.

*Maybe being seen and heard would be enough.
That would be a great start, in any case.*

Where do I find the people I need? Where have all the listeners gone? I know everyone is busy with their own lives and that meeting me where I am is going to require patience and energy.

I have figured out that if a person hasn't experienced significant loss, they can't have a hope of being with me in this. They simply can't get there.

I need someone who knows grief. I need someone like me.

Grief is a lonely road, but we were never meant to travel it alone. Loss is a universal experience. We all have people we care about leave, disappear, or die. Many of us are walking this demanding, unpredictable path. Finding fellow travelers can be a key to adjusting and living with loss.

We all need to be seen and heard, especially when we're hurting.

Usually, people who know grief are the ones who can see and relate to us the best. These people look into our eyes and sense our pain. They've been on this road. They know what it has been like for them, and they can better imagine what it might be like for us. They can do better than sympathize. They can empathize.

Yes, some fellow grievers are fixers and advice-givers. Some will compare their losses with ours and decide whose is worse or more difficult. Others, however, understand that there is no fixing this. They enter our lives with no agenda. On some level, they feel our pain and know that the best thing they can do is simply be with us. They offer us their presence.

These people are often found in support groups. Sometimes they are grief counselors or spiritual mentors. We need them, and they need us. We're in this together.

Affirmation: I will find people who will listen and walk this grief road with me.

I WANT TO LAY BLAME
SOMEWHERE

FROM THE GRIEVING HEART:

Today guilt came visiting again. I can't seem to shake it.

I get better for a while, and then a cloud descends. I feel responsible. I should have known. I should have said or done something more.

Is this just me trying to hold on to you somehow? Am I wanting to feel responsible? Is this my heart working overtime to make sense out of you leaving?

Yes, I feel guilty. There's a constant, dull pressure on my chest. Too much is unknown. I want to lay blame somewhere. I admit that guilt feels good sometimes. It gives my emotion a target, someplace to go.

All of this seems so big, and I feel so small. It's all above my pay grade and way beyond my abilities to resolve. I wish my heart would heal and be more at peace. I feel so unsteady and shaky right now.

In the end, I know feeling guilty doesn't help. It won't bring you back. Nothing will. Does anyone else feel this way?

Guilt often hides in the recesses of our hearts and pops up at the most inconvenient times. We think we've resolved things. We seem to have let go a little and forgiven ourselves for whatever we might have done or said, not done or not said. Then we wake up and find guilt hanging out in our living room. It smiles and begins its accusations all over again.

We said before that guilt will come knocking, repetitively. We can refuse to answer, but we can't stop it from making noise. It sneaks in when we're not aware. Before we know it, we're thinking those guilty, it's-all-my-fault thoughts again.

We could get discouraged with ourselves. We could get angry and swear that we'll never feel guilty again. We could venture down darker roads, assuming responsibility that isn't ours and wondering what punishment might fit us the best.

On the other hand, we can remind ourselves that this is the nature of guilt — it keeps knocking and popping up, again and again. When it comes, we can acknowledge this unwanted visitor and then release it. Release, release, and release again, as many times as necessary.

Grief is heavy enough without guilt attached to it. We breathe deeply. We tell ourselves that guilt's voice is not our own. We see it as the foreign invader it is and forgive ourselves yet again.

Affirmation: I'll release guilt and forgive myself as many times as necessary. Grief is heavy enough without allowing guilt to become my constant companion.

I'M IN CONTROL OF SO LITTLE

FROM THE GRIEVING HEART:

Yesterday, it was guilt. Today, it's anger. I'm back at it again. Surely someone somewhere is responsible for all this.

In the end, my mind figures that all the possible roads of blame end with God. At the end of the day, he's responsible, right? And yet, if he is good, how can he be responsible for tragedies, disasters, and evil? But if he is in control, then how is he not ultimately responsible for the pain and suffering in the world?

Your leaving has generated all kinds of questions, seemingly unsolvable riddles, and uncomfortable wonderings. I don't know how strong my faith was before all this, but now it feels shaky. I guess that's not surprising since I feel shaky. My whole world seems to be tottering. I feel so alone.

Perhaps no one is to blame. Maybe it's all coincidence and random. What about chance or fate? I don't know. I can't believe that my knowing you is random and simply by chance. That scares me more than all the other options.

One thing is certain. I'm in control of very little, and that's unnerving. I feel that I am at the whim of forces much greater than myself, and I don't know what to do with that.

The loss of a mate can create spiritual questioning. This is natural and common. Our world has been upended, and whatever we believed about life, ourselves, the universe, and God is undergoing an intense examination in our hearts and minds. If what we think or believe doesn't provide sufficient answers for what happened, we might be thrown into a crisis of faith.

We can find ourselves wondering what we believe, deep down inside where no one else can see. Most of us seek answers that will allow us to be more at peace with ourselves, with what happened, and with the world around us. Many of us are extremely uncomfortable with the unknown. We see mysteries as something to be solved and revealed, and not as unknowns to be lived with.

We hunger to know. We long to understand. But most of all, we hurt, because we dared to love.

Yes, we know that the mortality rate among humans is 100%. We are intellectually aware that one day we and all those who are important to us will die. But when a spouse leaves, these obvious facts of life come crashing in on us and we are undone by the power of loss.

At the end of the day, we are all human. Our hearts are resilient, yet incredibly fragile. We're wired for connection. When a strand of our life-web (especially this strand) is severed, everything shakes.

Our hearts and souls search for answers. We look for those we love.

Affirmation: What I believe might be shaken or undergo some intense examination. This is natural.

NOTHING SEEMS TO MATTER

FROM THE GRIEVING HEART:

On some days, like today, I don't want to do anything.

*I'm drained. Exhausted. Life feels so heavy. Nothing seems
to matter much. I find myself asking, "So what?"*

*What does it matter if I get up today and do
what I'm supposed to do? Who cares?*

*We chase after possessions and prestige. We climb whatever ladder is set in
front of us, struggling and competing to get to the top. And then what? Ultimately, we die. And we may lose anything and everything along the way up.*

*Life seems pointless at times. Maybe my heart is waving the white flag,
ready to surrender the battle of trying to make sense of your leaving and
this new, unwanted life I find myself in. I don't enjoy what I used to.
All is dull and drab. I have no motivation. I'm a big ball of do-nothing
and go-nowhere. I'm in a hole, and I want to crawl in deeper.*

*Apathetic. That's what I am. Am I going downhill here? Is this
temporary? Can I get out of this hole? Will I want to?*

Too many questions. No wonder I'm exhausted.

When life drains us, apathy is often not far behind. We simply don't
have the energy to care. All our resources have been shifted into survival
gear. Our systems are focused on maintaining enough equilibrium that

we can adjust, recover, and eventually heal over time. Our batteries have automatically switched into energy-saving mode.

No wonder we're not as motivated. It's enough of a battle to keep going and doing life from day to day without our spouses. Periods of loss and heavy emotion are typically not a time for making big decisions and trying to move ahead. This season is one of grief. And grief is necessary to process and heal from a loss, especially the loss of a mate.

At some point, it's healthy if we consider and alter our expectations of ourselves to fit where we are. Our main agenda is to guard our hearts and grieve in as healthy a way as possible. All else is secondary. As we grieve well, the rest of life will fall into place over time.

For now, the goal is to be patient with ourselves, others, and our current routine. We might feel pointless, meaningless, and apathetic. We might feel like we're stuck in a pit with no way out. As we grieve, this will change.

Thankfully, now is not forever.

Affirmation: Even if I feel empty and apathetic, I'll be patient with myself. I trust that this will change over time.

I'M GETTING TIRED
OF FAKING IT

FROM THE GRIEVING HEART:

I feel depressed. No wonder. Life is depressing right now.

I'm not myself. I used to smile. Now, smiling is just a show, a facade. I'm beginning to tire of this counterfeit lifestyle I seem to be living in public. Performing and holding it together for everyone else takes way too much energy.

There are times I want to bust out, forget what's acceptable, and shout how I really feel about all this.

"How are you?" people ask. "Well, I'm not fine. I'm angry, frustrated, and hurt. I'm sad, depressed, and lonely. I'm confused, anxious, and afraid. I'm grieving."

It would feel so good to say that. Why can't I?

I guess I think it would only make things worse. I'm already being treated like I have an infectious disease. People avoid me. It's obvious they don't know what to do with me. Honestly, I don't know what to do with myself either.

So, I hide. I keep it inside. No wonder I feel depressed.

In times of loss, feeling depressed is natural and common. When a spouse departs, the effects can be devastating. Our hearts are feeling the extent of the loss. We're tired, even exhausted. Our emotions are heavy and oppressive. We don't feel like ourselves. We can't function as we've become accustomed to. Putting one foot in front of the other takes more out of us than we would have ever dreamed.

We look at the past and long for it. We look ahead, and all is hazy. We've had other losses, but we've never been here before. Everything has changed somehow. Feeling depressed is a natural response for a shattered heart.

Perhaps we can find a little relief if we remember that most depression in grief is temporary and situational. It's not where we were or where we will be, but it's where we are now. This is part of love. We feel our mate's absence. It hurts. Our hearts crack. Our bodies feel the tumultuous onslaught of our grief. Our souls are hit with the pain.

Accepting ourselves, even when depressed, is important. Others may not understand, which makes it even more crucial to give ourselves a break.

We are where we are. As we grieve, our emotions will change over time.

Affirmation: I will accept myself and trust that any depression I experience is temporary and will pass with time.

FOR REFLECTION
AND/OR JOURNALING

My Grieving Heart:
*"As I learn to live without your physical presence, some ways
that I can express my love and honor you are..."*

_____

_____

_____

_____

_____

_____

_____

_____

_____

_____

_____

_____

_____

_____

_____

_____

_____

_____

_____

_____

_____

_____

_____

_____

_____

_____

_____

_____

_____

_____

_____

_____

_____

FOR REFLECTION
AND/OR JOURNALING

My Grieving Heart:
"As I learn to live without your physical presence, some ways that I can express my love and honor you are..."

_____

_____

_____

_____

_____

_____

_____

_____

_____

_____

_____

_____

_____

_____

I MISS EVERYTHING

FROM THE GRIEVING HEART:

I miss you.

I miss your voice, your presence, and your laughter. I miss your smile, your eyes, and your touch.

I miss everything. I love you.

I wonder if this intense sadness, this depression I'm experiencing, will ever get better. What if it goes on and on? What if I don't feel better? What if all this gets the better of me and I end up living as a shell of a person for the rest of my life?

What if this pit I'm in becomes my home? What if the depression stays, and becomes my life?

Just the thought of it is terrifying. Life looks so dark and dreary. It's hard to imagine this cloud lifting. I've forgotten what joy feels like.

I don't like this. Loss is terrible. Missing you is worse than I could have ever dreamed. In fact, my life is becoming a perpetual nightmare without you.

I want to be out of this pit and feel the sunlight and breeze on my face again. I want to live. Have I forgotten how?

In grief, it is common for us to assume that the way things are now is how they will be. We can see the past, but our future has been altered and disrupted. If we're experiencing depression, we naturally wonder how long this will continue.

Is this grief more than for a season? Is this our new life? Will we be able to get out of this pit?

If our depression deepens to the point where we don't go out, don't get out of bed, and don't function in daily life, it's possible that something more than temporary situational depression is at work. This isn't only about our loss, but it is also influenced by our current situation, including our physical condition, financial stability, relational support network, and overall mental and emotional health. Other recent losses or major life changes can also complicate things.

If we become isolated and non-functional for two weeks or more, it's time to reach out and seek professional help. Grief counselors, therapists, physicians, and clergy are often sought for their expertise during these times. If we're having suicidal thoughts, the temptation is to keep this to ourselves. This is the last thing we should do. If self-harm is part of our thought life, it's best to call 911 or seek help immediately.

There is no shame in seeking help. Reaching out is wise and is part of taking our own hearts seriously.

Affirmation: If my depression deepens, I'll reach out
for help. This is part of loving myself, and you.

WHY DO PEOPLE SAY SUCH THINGS?

FROM THE GRIEVING HEART:

Why do people feel like they have to compare? It seems like everyone wants to compare their losses to mine.

"My mom passed away ten years ago, so I know how you feel."

"I lost a friend in high school, and it was much worse than this."

"You think you're hurting? I've lost five people in the last two years."

"You think this is bad? It only gets worse."

Why do people say such things? All people are not the same. Every relationship is different. They didn't lose you. They can't see and know my heart or my pain. What do they know?

We all need to express our grief. I get that. But why do we have to play the comparison game while we grieve?

~~~

As human beings, we tend to compare. We wonder how we're doing, or how we're supposed to be doing, so we look around and evaluate. When we start to compare emotional pain, however, we're in dangerous territory.

Grieving hearts don't need to be evaluated, but rather they should be seen and heard. We need connection, not comparison. When others make our pain about them and their grief, we naturally feel invisible or even belittled.

It would be nice if we could meet each other where we are and express kindness. Honestly, listening and expressing compassion is often easier than living a self-focused, self-centered life. Our hearts long for mutual relationships. Having someone thrust themselves upon us is a boundary violation that does not sit well with our souls.

Words matter. Words can hurt. And yet, we can't afford to let unfeeling statements of comparison rule our minds and hearts. If we're willing, we can use unhelpful statements like those above as fuel for our grief fire. We can find ways to process our emotions about these encounters in ways that allow us to empty a little bit of our grief reservoir.

Comparison never benefits anyone. It can steal our identity and keep joy far from us.

Affirmation: I'll find ways to express my grief without comparing my loss to that of others. Comparison does not help me grieve well.

I DON'T LIKE THIS NEW LIFE

FROM THE GRIEVING HEART:

I don't like this new life. I want a life with you back in it. I miss talking to you. I want to hear your voice — not a voicemail, but your real voice. I want to feel your touch. I want you here, now.

I get so frustrated I want to scream. Yesterday, I did. I didn't even realize it. I let it rip, right in my bedroom. It felt so good, I screamed again, this time into my pillow. That felt good too, but not near as satisfying as letting it fill the air, full force.

I have so much inside me. I think it builds up over time. That makes sense. I hide so much just to be able to be around people and get through the day. I stuff more than I realize. I need a pressure release from time to time and screaming seems to fit the bill.

I can feel the emotion welling up inside, moving from my torso and up into my throat. I've been slamming the door shut on it since you left. No more. I'm going to scream. If I'm around people, I'll excuse myself and head to the car. I'm betting the car would make a good screaming place.

Life was already crazy. With you gone, it's even more nuts. When I think about screaming, I smile.

Smiling feels good.

Finding healthy ways to grieve while remaining functional can be challenging. After all, there were two of us. Now, there's only one.

For most, it's natural to want to hole up and grieve quietly on our own. As time goes by, the grief inside begins to build up. Our internal grief reservoir rises. Sooner or later, we need space to allow it to overflow.

Many grieving spouses find screaming to be a great way to release pent-up tension and emotion. Some scream into pillows. Some scream in their cars. I know a swimmer who screams underwater in the pool. Expressing the powerful emotions in short bursts can be effective and relieving. Periodically, we need to air what's inside.

Grief will be expressed, one way or another. Better to let it out in healthy ways than to force it to leak out in ways we might later regret.

Some things are worth screaming about. The loss of a mate is certainly one of those.

Affirmation: Life is tough and losing you is painful. There's plenty to scream about.

I'M MISSING THE FUTURE

FROM THE GRIEVING HEART:

I have been missing the past. Now, I'm missing the future.

I'm missing my future with you in it. You won't be there. You won't be here on your birthday. Or my birthday. You'll be absent at Thanksgiving, Christmas, and every other holiday. Every special day we had will now consist of just me and my memories of you.

I've not only lost you, I've lost the future I was anticipating. Everything is different, and so is the future.

I thought I knew who I was, what I was doing and where I was going. Now, I'm not so sure. Every thought and picture I had of the future was about us. Now there is only empty space where you would have been.

Sounds strange to say I need to grieve a lost future. Yet, that's reality. I miss what I had. I miss what I anticipated. I miss you.

I know I will somehow make it through this, but I don't like it at all.

When a life partner departs, our world changes, and that includes the future. What we anticipated will be significantly altered. What we planned on may be no more. The closer our relationship with our mates, the more deeply our lives will be affected going forward.

When hit by this devastating loss, we not only grieve what we had but also what we will not have in the future. Unfortunately, along the way we discover other losses that are also connected to our partners – relationships, activities, holidays, traditions, etc. It's never about just the one loss but includes all the other strands of our life-web.

People are important. Life is about relationships. When a spouse exits, the future we had envisioned changes. With each holiday or special event, we become hyper-aware of who's missing. Our grief surfaces, and powerful emotions can hijack us at a moment's notice.

Though the future is now different, it can still be good. We can help make it good by taking our hearts seriously and grieving well. Of course, we miss them and wish they were here. Perhaps we can't imagine the road ahead without them. That's okay. The answers we need will come when our hearts are ready for them.

Affirmation: It's hard to imagine a future without you in it. I will focus on grieving well and celebrating you along the way.

I'M TIRED OF GRIEF

FROM THE GRIEVING HEART:

I don't like the looks I'm getting. Maybe I'm being too sensitive or seeing what's not there, but it feels like people are tired of me and my grief.

I'm tired of my grief too, but it's not like I can wish it away. The emotions rattle inside me, like some ricocheting superball – back and forth, up and down. I'm exhausted. I can't think, and yet my mind is spinning. I sleep but can't seem to rest.

Yes, I'm tired of grief. I'm tired, period.

I know that being with someone who's grieving is not the easiest thing in the world. Perhaps it's frustrating and draining. If so, no wonder people don't want to be around me. They all just want me to feel better.

I get that. I want me to feel better too. I wish I could.

But right now, I hurt. I can't seem to hide it, either. My grief spills out, unbidden and unwanted.

I'm still a mess.

Grief can wear us out. After a while, our energy reserves begin to be depleted. Our ability and desire to hold our grief in check may dwindle. Sadness, anger, and frustration begin to ooze out of our pores and onto the world around us.

People who love us are naturally concerned. It's hard for us and difficult for them. Watching us hurt and suffer isn't easy for them, but it's where we are at the moment.

Being able to accept another person for where they are at any given time is both a gift and a skill. Some people seem to do this naturally and almost effortlessly. Others grow so uncomfortable with grief and its emotions that they either try to pull us out of where we are or distance themselves from us. It's a challenging place to be, for everyone.

And it's especially difficult for those of us with shattered hearts and broken dreams.

We want to feel better. We wish we could. Some days are okay. Others are dark and painful. Getting through the day can require all we've got.

The best we can do is be ourselves, as much as possible. We grieve and let the chips fall where they may. Others' responses are their own. It's not our job to take care of those around us emotionally. They must do that for themselves.

We breathe deeply, forgive quickly, and grieve.

Affirmation: I can't control the words and actions of others. I'll focus on grieving and being the best me possible in this situation.

FOR REFLECTION
AND/OR JOURNALING

My Grieving Heart:
*"So far, here are some things I'm learning
on this grief journey:"*

_____

_____

_____

_____

_____

_____

_____

_____

_____

_____

_____

_____

_____

_____

_____

_____

_____

_____

_____

_____

_____

_____

_____

_____

_____

_____

_____

_____

_____

_____

_____

I'M LONELY

People seem shy around me. And no one mentions you. Why is that?

Are they worried about upsetting me? I'm already upset.

Are they concerned about me tearing up and grieving? Don't they know I'm already grieving and can't help it?

Do they not want me to think about you? Don't they know you're always in my heart and never far from my mind?

Have they forgotten you? Don't they know I can't?

They may not talk about you, but I will. I will speak your name. I will say it out loud and often – a hundred times in a row if I want.

You are the invisible elephant in every room. Why can't we talk about you? Why can't we share what we miss and what you meant to us? Why can't we grieve together?

Maybe I'm unrealistic. Perhaps this is simply the way the world works. People leave, and life goes on. I can't expect others to get it or understand. It would be nice if they were sensitive and mentioned your name from time to time, but that's up to them.

Grief is lonely. I'm lonely.

I hope this gets better, eventually.

There might be people who mention our spouses and share what they miss about them, but chances are these people will be few. Most will express sympathy at first, and then promptly go on with their lives.

We're stunned, immobilized, and trying to figure out what happened, why, and what it means. It's almost as if we relocated to a new life. The world looks familiar, yet everything has changed. All of life feels different. It would be nice if others accepted this, but we certainly can't expect them to understand it.

We can't wait around for others to mention our mates' names and ask about them. We must take our own hearts seriously and begin speaking their names as often and as loudly as we need to. We courageously begin to share stories and memories with others. We encourage others to mention our spouses and share with us what they miss about them.

As we bravely speak their names, we give ourselves and others a chance to grieve. We present them with an invitation to join us in our grief. It might be emotionally uncomfortable, but it can be good and healing. Perhaps some will distance themselves, and that's okay. We must grieve. It's where we are.

We will speak their names. Often.

Affirmation: Even if others don't mention you, I will. I'll give us a chance to grieve together.

I WANT COMPANIONSHIP

FROM THE GRIEVING HEART:

*I miss you. I miss your presence, your touch, your voice.
Most of all, I miss your companionship.*

Time. I miss time with you. I feel so lonely.

*I'm beginning to want companionship. I'm conflicted
about this. My emotions are all over the place.*

*I know it's natural to want this. At least, I think it is. On the
other hand, I feel unfaithful for even thinking about it.*

*Part of me says, "What's the harm? Try it. Get together with someone and
just talk." Another part of me is terrified. How do I do this? With whom?*

*Others I talk with encourage me to go ahead, but I don't know.
They want me to feel better. They want me to move on. They
have no idea how complicated this is for my heart.*

*My heart is giving me conflicting messages. I miss you and so I'm
willing to go and talk to someone else? Weird. It's all so strange.*

Why did you have to go?

We're designed for connection. We're relational creatures. We attach. We seek to love and be loved. We need interaction, acceptance, and a sense of belonging. We need to be seen, heard, and known.

We experienced all this with our mates. Now they're gone, and we're left with what feels like nothing. Our closest, most intimate companionship has been removed from our lives. Our life-web has all the same strands, but yet it is nothing like it was before.

To want companionship is natural, healthy, and human.

If we choose to seek this, we need to decide what our boundaries will be beforehand. If we initiate a meeting with someone, we need to let them know what those boundaries are. We must be honest with ourselves, our own hearts, and the other person.

Each step forward in our healing and recovery takes guts. Growth demands courage. There is risk in reaching out for companionship. We don't know what kind of reaction we'll get. We don't know how this is going to go. We don't know exactly what to say or do.

If the invitation comes to us, as will often be the case, we might at first be shocked and not know how to respond. We can take our time. No need to feel pressure.

"I didn't expect that. Can I get back to you?"

"Thank you for asking. This is a strange time for me. Let me think about it."

If we know we're not ready, it's best to simply be honest. Clear, direct communication is important at these times. Life is muddled enough already. Don't try to protect the other person's heart. Just be yourself, be kind, and be honest, and you'll automatically be protecting their heart and yours.

We continue breathing deeply. We can take our time. Hasty decisions are rarely wise, especially during times of loss and grief.

Affirmation: If asked for companionship, I'll respond kindly
and honestly. I'll take my time. My heart is at stake.

I'M EVEN MORE VULNERABLE THAN I THOUGHT

FROM THE GRIEVING HEART:

I'm more vulnerable than I thought.

I view myself as a fairly strong, competent individual. Losing you has shaken that.

Suddenly, I'm wondering about a lot. Things that I didn't even consider before now bother me -- and even frighten me.

I'm skittish about relationships. All relationships. I wonder what people are thinking. I don't know what to say or how to act. And when I'm approached by someone who expresses interest in me, I'm flattered and terrified at the same time.

I've heard horror stories from others who have lost spouses. Many have gone out with people who are interested in what they can get. They feel used. And sometimes this happens even with people that they know.

I now know why some seek companionship online. It feels safer somehow. They're not in the same room. I would have more control over what I say and how I respond. But I hear tragic stories about online communication too.

I feel shaky. I want companionship, but is that just because I'm missing you?

We feel more vulnerable after losing a life partner. That's because we are more vulnerable - in almost every area.

Vulnerability is not necessarily a negative thing. It's a natural result of losing a mate. Our hearts have been hit. Our lives have been upended. Our worlds have been altered forever. Life is not business as usual, and we are not the people we once were.

Loneliness becomes our constant companion, even if we're surrounded all day long by other people. We're now walking with a pronounced limp, if we can walk at all. There's a massive hole in our hearts.

Relationships are normally complicated. When we're in grief, they tend to be even more so. How we handle requests for companionship or dates is important for the health of our hearts.

Sadly, there are some who would take advantage of our vulnerability. Relationships always come with the risk of things not working out. In our current state of emotional pain, the last thing we want is to feel used.

When we're grieving and vulnerable, we're most susceptible to options that promise relief and distraction. We want to feel better. Some are willing to launch out and take risks that they normally wouldn't. Depending on the hearts involved and the situation, this can be healthy and good, or not.

When in doubt, we take our time. Waiting is not a bad thing, though most of us don't do it well. Patience isn't common in our digital age. Grief, recovery, and healing take time. When we're ready, we can take the next step, whatever that is.

While we're grieving, it's best to take only one step a time rather than leaping ahead. Impulsive decisions and sudden, radical choices rarely work out well for grieving hearts.

We breathe deeply. We can take our time. We don't need to make anything happen. Good is all around us. Hope is always here. As we're patient, the next step will become visible.

Affirmation: I'm lonely, and that's okay. I'll take my time and trust that I'll know what the next step is when it's time.

SILENCE, LISTENING EARS, AND A HUG CAN DO WONDERS

FROM THE GRIEVING HEART:

*Yesterday a good friend said, "Well, at least you knew
him as long as you did. You were blessed."*

Yes, I'm blessed to have known you. But I wanted you longer. Much longer.

*It reminds me of another statement last week, when a co-worker
hugged me and stated, "At least he is in a better place now."*

I agree, but I want you here, now.

Anything beginning with "At least…" is void of any comfort to me at all.

*I'm ashamed to remember that I've used my share of "At least…" statements
in the past. "At least they're not suffering anymore." "At least you had a
wonderful relationship." "At least you have a good, supportive family."*

*I didn't know what to say. I guess I thought I had
to say something. I know better now.*

A little silence, listening ears, and a hug can do wonders.

When someone experiences the loss of a mate, no one knows what to say.
There are no words for such things. All verbal attempts to fix, encourage,
or somehow make things better fall to the ground with little or no fruit.

We've all been recipients of some at-least statements. Though some of these might be true, few are comforting. Grieving hearts need to be seen, heard, and understood, and these statements come across more as platitudes. We spout them off without thinking how the grieving heart in front of us might hear it.

Yes, these statements will come. People don't know what to say, so they tend to say what they've heard in similar situations. Of course, we would be better served if those around us spent less time talking and more time listening to our hearts and souls. Though it sounds simple, this requires time, patience, and a willingness to be in the presence of emotional suffering. In our world, convenience is king, and there is nothing convenient about loss and grief.

We all need to be seen and heard. People who are acquainted with grief and with whom we feel safe are our best bet. And if we've said things we now regret to other grieving hearts in the past, it's time to forgive ourselves. We're now in a different place. Now we know this pain, and we're much better equipped to engage with and comfort other grieving hearts.

A little silence, listening ears, and a hug can indeed do wonders. Our hearts heal moment by moment and piece by piece when we give away what we need.

Affirmation: Since I now know grief, I can engage with other grieving hearts. This could be good for both of us.

I HAD NO IDEA

FROM THE GRIEVING HEART:

I've been thinking more about my responses in the past when I encountered those who were grieving. I feel sad about my lack of compassion. I didn't know. I couldn't have known.

Until I lost you, I had no idea what this kind of pain was like. I thought I could imagine a bit, and maybe put myself in others' shoes. Now, I know such thinking is arrogant. How could I know without having been there?

When others lost loved ones, I was sympathetic for a while. But honestly, I expected them to be back to normal quickly. And I expected them to be the same people they were before.

Ridiculous.

Losing you has broken my heart. Now, I can recognize other broken hearts. Loss and grief have made life more real and each day more important. For these things, I'm grateful.

There are many grieving hearts out there, more than I could ever know.

Until we encounter significant loss, we tend to be quick to judge. We march along our daily routine, comparing ourselves with others. We always come out ahead or short. We evaluate others and ourselves. Above all, we avoid being uncomfortable. Loss, grief, and the accompanying emotions can be unnerving.

Now that we know terrible, heavy loss, our hearts are more sensitive. We know what brokenness and the loneliness of loss feel like. We can now empathize as well as sympathize. We can bring comfort to other grieving hearts because we know grief.

Some of us might like our alone time, but no one enjoys feeling alone. We're wired for relationship and hunger for connection more than most of us realize. Grief might separate us from some people we've known, but it can also connect us to others. These new connections can be deep and meaningful.

Grieving is hard, exhausting work. Every day can be a battle. We need comrades for this fight — people we can trust and count on. We can be those people for other grieving hearts, if we're willing. We can be comforters, even while hurting. And this can bring a new sense of meaning to our pain and suffering.

We're in this together, and we need each other — badly.

Affirmation: Even though I'm hurting, I can comfort others. My pain has purpose.

FOR REFLECTION
AND/OR JOURNALING

MY GRIEVING HEART:
*"Since my mate departed, I have felt
more vulnerable when…"*

_____

_____

_____

_____

_____

_____

_____

_____

_____

_____

_____

_____

_____

_____

_____

_____

_____

_____

_____

_____

_____

_____

_____

_____

_____

_____

_____

_____

_____

_____

_____

FOR REFLECTION
AND/OR JOURNALING

MY GRIEVING HEART:
*"Since my mate departed, I have felt
more vulnerable when…"*

_____

_____

_____

_____

_____

_____

_____

_____

_____

_____

_____

_____

_____

_____

_____

_____

_____

_____

_____

_____

_____

_____

_____

_____

_____

_____

_____

_____

_____

_____

_____

_____

GET OVER YOU? IMPOSSIBLE.

FROM THE GRIEVING HEART:

*My own family doesn't understand. I thought that they, of
all people, would be compassionate and helpful.*

*Don't get me wrong. Some relatives have been great. They're not me, and
so they don't understand entirely, but they're respectful. They don't evaluate how I'm doing or try to fix me. They simply love me where I am.*

*Others, however, are sending the message, "Aren't
you over this by now? Buck up."*

Get over you? No. Impossible.

*The fact that this comes from family hurts even more. Fam-
ily members are supposed to be safe, right? I guess people are, well,
people. We seem to be basically selfish and most interested in what's
comfortable and pleasant for us. But it's still disappointing.*

*I'm grateful for supportive relatives. I can entrust my heart and emo-
tions to them. With the others, I'll guard my heart and try to extend the
understanding and compassion to them that they seem unable to give me. I
will not let unkind responses take control of or overly influence my heart.*

Our media seems fascinated with suffering, tragedy, and death. We report the shocking and the unthinkable. But when grief enters our own
backyard, we tend to bar the door quickly.

Most of us naturally expect family to love and support us amid difficulty. Some families are super-supportive in tough times, while others are not. Usually, there are a few sympathetic, loving souls in our family circle. We can be grateful for their support and help. And there will be other relatives who simply don't do well in the presence of emotional pain and grief.

We never get over a person. That's impossible. When a spouse dies or departs, we're crushed. Our hearts are struck. When this strand of our life-web is severed, it's often traumatic. Over time, we begin to decipher who is helpful to us in our grief and who is not.

One of our biggest challenges is to spend time with those who are helpful and supportive while limiting our exposure to those who aren't.

We don't get over people – especially soulmates. We don't cease to love. We simply get through this time as best we can.

Affirmation: With family, I'll open my heart to those who are supportive, and limit my exposure to those who aren't.

I FEEL YOU SLIPPING AWAY

FROM THE GRIEVING HEART:

*My mind moves so quickly. My heart is a jumble.
My emotions are all over the place.*

*I thought I would be better by now. I don't know what I mean by
that exactly. Maybe I think I should be feeling less, be less upset, be
more stable, or be functioning better. It would be nice to be more
than a nanosecond away from being a blithering, sobbing idiot.*

*I don't know what I expected, but this is a longer and
harder road than I could have ever imagined.*

I miss you. No wonder I feel this way.

*I feel scattered and distracted. I can't seem to focus. My con-
centration is virtually nil. What is happening to me?*

*I know. It's grief. Losing you is what's happening to me. In
some senses, I lose you again and again, day after day.*

*My life seems like it's in slow motion, yet I sense I need to slow
down somehow. I need to slow down my mind and my heart. I
can't seem to grasp much of what is happening in my life.*

I feel like I can't breathe. My soul needs more oxygen.

Grief is tough. Loss is painful. We naturally wonder how long this uncomfortable season will last. Most of us want to feel better as quickly as
possible.

Our world is fast-paced. We're not used to waiting. We grumble at red lights. We sigh when a web page takes more than a second to load. We expect everything quickly, if not instantly.

Love and relationships operate according to different time schedules. Building the strands of our life-web takes time, energy, and work. Marriage is a special, unique, and powerful bond. Grieving the loss of a spouse can be a long process.

Grief is not a sprint. It's a marathon roller-coaster that endlessly repeats. Over time, we get used to the ups, the downs, and getting thrown around emotionally. Our bruised hearts get bumped again and again. At times, we wince and writhe with the pain. The dull ache of loss seems to permeate our lives.

Grief requires great patience. Accepting ourselves is difficult. Processing all the different facets of our loss is demanding and exhausting. Recovering and adjusting are processes, not destinations.

We must be patient with ourselves. We live in a new world now. The terrain is unfamiliar and the path uncertain. Taking our hearts seriously, moment by moment, is our new priority.

Affirmation: Grieving is a process. I'll be patient
with myself and accept myself along the way.

I'LL NEVER FORGET
YOU, WILL I?

FROM THE GRIEVING HEART:

I miss you.

I know I'll never forget you, but I find myself concerned that I'll be less connected to you in the future. Strange. I fear losing you, even though you are gone.

My mind knows that my sense of closeness to you will most likely diminish as time marches on. It hurts to think about this. You're slowly slipping away from me. I can feel it.

I listen to voicemails to remember what your voice sounds like. I look at pictures to remind myself of the features of your face. If it's this way now, what about a year down the road? Will there be a time when I no longer think of you?

Silly as it sounds, I'm worried about forgetting you. I'm scared you will slowly fade from my mind and heart.

Perhaps I need to speak your name more often. Maybe I need to be bold and share memories more than I do. I don't know.

I do know this: I love you.

As time passes, our grief tends to change. For most, the emotions grow less intense and debilitating. The loss settles into our hearts in new ways and often a persistent, dull ache invades us. We might find ourselves thinking about our spouse less.

Absence only makes the heart grow fonder to a certain extent. Experiencing connection and closeness requires a person's presence, time, and communication. When a mate departs, we can slowly lose our sense of them. We're stunned one day to find ourselves wondering what their voice sounded like. We can become frightened of losing them completely. We sense them slipping away from us, bit by bit.

Soon after the loss, we might be obsessed with our partners and our memories of them. We're thinking about them constantly. What they did and said. Their voice and their laughter. Our times with them, good and bad. Our heart is focused, and everything is about them.

As we grieve, emotion is released. Our hearts process the loss over time. We slowly begin to adjust. The loss becomes a part of our lives. Our souls begin to grapple with a life without our spouse's physical presence.

We will never forget them. They have an always-place in our hearts. But our sense of them will change over time. This is part of healing.

Affirmation: If I feel less connected to you,
I won't panic. This is part of grief.

I MUST TALK ABOUT YOU

FROM THE GRIEVING HEART:

You feel more distant now. I know this is natural, but I don't like it.

I don't like any of this. I want you back.

I will not forget you. I won't let that happen. I will speak your name, out loud and often. I will talk about you to anyone who will listen. I don't care what they think. I don't care if they think I'm weak or crazy. So what if they look at me and roll their eyes?

I must talk about you. I must find people who will listen.

I will remember and find ways to honor you. I will go on with you, with your influence inside me.

Yet, almost every day I'm saying goodbye to you somehow. Ugh.

You would want me to live and live well. Perhaps living and grieving well is a way I can still love you.

As times goes on, most of us feel more distant from our departed mates. This is natural and common. They are no longer in front of us and their absence is becoming part of our new normal.

Many feel they need to say goodbye, slowly and over a period of time, in order to engage in life again. Others resist this, choosing to focus on remembering. Still others refuse to let go in any sense, clinging to any and every thought, memory, or possession that helps keep their spouse alive in their minds and hearts.

Loss is universal. We all experience it. But grief is deeply personal. Each relationship is unique, and each heart's grief will be unique as well. There is no standard, one-size-fits-all path. We must each find our own way.

Remembering is a part of grieving. Speaking our partners' names and telling their stories can be a wonderful way to share ourselves and our hearts with those around us. Finding those we can do this with is important – even essential – to our emotional and physical health.

We will speak their names. We will tell their stories. We will live on, with their influence inside us.

Affirmation: I will speak your name and tell your story – our story. This helps me grieve and is part of loving myself and you.

I'M TIRED OF BEING AFRAID

FROM THE GRIEVING HEART:

I know this sounds morbid, but I find myself wondering, again, who's next?

I don't allow myself to think about this, much less voice it. But deep in a corner of my brain, a fear is lurking. I'm waiting for the next loss. If this could happen to you, then it could happen to anyone, anywhere, at any time.

It could happen to me. Am I next?

I don't like these sad and depressing thoughts. But it's true. Anyone. Anywhere. Any time. Even me, or someone else I love and care about.

I find myself wanting to wrap everyone I see in bubble-wrap and lock everyone I care about away in some impenetrable vault. I want to go where no one leaves and nothing bad can happen to anyone.

Reality is hard. I want things to be good again. I want to feel joy and maybe a little peace. I'm tired of worrying and being afraid.

Fear is common and natural in times of loss. Our world has been up-ended. Our life-web has been shaken. Our hearts have been jostled. Life has changed. The unknown has reared its ugly head. We wonder about a lot of things.

One loss can lead us to fear another. After a horrific auto accident, it would be natural to not want to drive for a while. Perhaps we get nervous just thinking about getting in a car. We naturally worry about another crash.

In grief, we often come face to face with our own mortality and that of all those we love. If we've had enough loss and tragedy in the past, we can find ourselves waiting for the next disaster to strike. We begin to do life in fortress mode, trying to protect ourselves and those around us from more loss.

Of course, living in fear is not really living. We can learn to acknowledge fear when it comes and release it. We might have to release it again and again. As we grieve, our hearts will process all this, and there will come a day when we're willing to get back in the car again.

As we grieve in healthy ways, we will adjust and heal. We will never be the same. On some level, we might always grieve. We learn to live on while grieving.

Affirmation: When the fear of more loss comes, I'll acknowledge the fear and release it. This is part of grieving and living well.

FOR REFLECTION
AND/OR JOURNALING

MY GRIEVING HEART:
"When I think about companionship and possibly dating again, I…"

_____

_____

_____

_____

_____

_____

_____

_____

_____

_____

_____

_____

_____

_____

_____

_____

_____

_____

_____

_____

_____

_____

_____

_____

_____

_____

_____

_____

_____

_____

_____

_____

I THOUGHT I WAS BETTER

FROM THE GRIEVING HEART:

I thought I was doing better. Then I saw an ad for one of our favorite movies. It struck my heart like lightning. For a moment, I was stunned…paralyzed. Then the flood of sadness poured out of me.

I felt as if I had lost you all over again.

Is this ever going to end? Why can't I control myself?

Am I making progress, or going backward? Am I stuck?

I know I've said this kind of thing before – probably a dozen times, if not more.

I don't think I'm stuck. I just feel lost at times. I feel a little stronger…and then discover I'm still a mess.

I guess that's the grief roller-coaster. I think things have leveled out, and then I suddenly find myself being whipped around again.

Patience. Yes. Grief requires patience. I must be patient with myself. I'm worth that. You would want that.

Breathe. Again. One breath at a time. One moment at a time.

Grief is such a back-and-forth, up-and-down emotional process that we can get turned around. We wonder which end is up. What does progress look like? Will there ever be a stable routine again?

After a while, our emotions might level out. Life gets a tad bit smoother. Then we get hit with another grief burst. Another anvil whacks us out of a clear blue sky. We're shocked and stunned all over again. The grief feels so familiar that we can end up believing we're back where we started.

Nothing could be further from the truth.

Grief bursts will come. Triggers are everywhere. Our heart wounds can be poked by anything, anytime, anywhere. As we've said before, we can't protect ourselves from these sudden intrusions, but we can decide beforehand how we will handle them. We can let the grief come. It's natural and healthy. We can feel the emotions, as we are able. Some talk out loud about what's happening inside them.

Others process these bursts through writing. Still others share with safe people they trust.

Again, these grief bursts are common and normal. They will come. They will go. Our hearts are remembering. Our emotions are declaring our love.

Being kind to ourselves by being patient with ourselves is vital.

Affirmation: When grief bursts come, I will breathe deeply and feel them through. These times are steps forward, not backward.

I DREAD SPECIAL DAYS

FROM THE GRIEVING HEART:

One of our special days is coming up. I can feel the dread as it approaches.

I want to remember you and grieve well on that day. I want to honor you.

I've decided to write you a letter telling you how I'm doing and what I miss about you, about me, and about us. I know it will be emotional, but I believe it will be good. I feel a little shy…but determined.

You're not here, but I still love you. I will express that love, as I can, when I can.

Maybe as time goes on, I will dread these special days less. Perhaps I can use them well and eventually they will bring joy instead of sadness. I choose to believe so.

I guess I could write a letter to you any day, couldn't I? I don't know why I didn't think of that before.

I'm thinking of you and smiling. That feels good.

We all have special days. These might be recognized holidays, or simply times that have significance for us and our relationship with our departed spouses. In any case, it's good to be aware of these days and prepare for them.

Many choose to do something meaningful to honor their mates on these days. Writing letters can be effective as this focuses our attention and slows down our distracted minds and hearts. We can express ourselves specifically and intentionally. Even if no one else reads it, our hearts have expressed themselves in a proactive and healthy way.

Making a simple plan for special days can help us prepare and relieve a lot of potential angst. It's helpful to be able to express what's inside us somehow. Writing, drawing, painting, sculpting, and talking out loud are possibilities. Giving a donation in their name, serving somewhere in their honor, or continuing a tradition they enjoyed are also good options.

As we grieve, we can find ways to make these days not only more bearable but good. Tears will be shed, but there will be smiles too.

Affirmation: Rather than dreading special days,
I will make plans to remember and honor you.
This is part of loving myself and you.

I NEED TO BE REAL

FROM THE GRIEVING HEART:

Writing that letter was good for me. I cried,
smiled, and laughed. I'm glad I did it.

In fact, I'm going to start writing more often. I guess people call that a jour-
nal. I don't want a diary. I'm not interested in simply recording where I went
and what I did. I want to express my heart. I'm eager to process this grief.

I'll begin by simply talking about what's happening inside me – what I'm
thinking and feeling. I'm guessing there's no right or wrong way to do this.
Giving my heart a safe place to vent is what's most important to me.

I have some safe people I can talk to, but even then, I hold back a
little. I don't want to be too shocking. When I write, I feel freer to
be me. As I express my heart, I'm struck again by the depth of my
love for you. Grieving your loss is more like running a cross country
race rather than a 100-yard dash. Even though I can't see the fin-
ish line, I'm beginning to run the race with more confidence.
I want to make you proud. I will win this race for "us".

When I write, I can be real. I need to be real.

Many have found keeping a journal to be a key to their recovery and
adjustment after the loss of a life partner. We can express thoughts and
emotions honestly and openly. There are things we might never be able
to say in front of another person, but we can get them down on paper.

In grief, getting things out is important. Expressing what's inside is crucial. Writing can help us do this.

Some can easily record what's happening inside, while others need more direction. Many find writing prompts to be helpful. Here are some examples:

- What I miss most today is…
- I find myself most concerned about…
- One of my fondest memories of you is…
- Things that have surprised me about grief are…
- If I could go back, I would…
- Some of the things I learned from you are…
- When I think about the future, I wonder…

There is no end to the possible prompts that could be used. Our hearts heal as they express themselves, bit by bit, over time. A journal is one more way we can speak their names, tell their stories, and honor them.

Affirmation: My heart needs to continually express itself
to be healthy and to heal. I'll find a way to do this.

MY HEART IS CHANGING

FROM THE GRIEVING HEART:

My heart is changing. Things that used to be important aren't anymore. Nothing matters except people.

As I look back, my biggest regrets involve relationships. Something I said. Something I did. Things I wish I could do over.

I have hurt others, and others have hurt me. My heart has wounds. Every heart does.

We don't talk about these wounds much. I guess we just live with them and hope that somehow everything will work out okay. My problem is that my wounds keep getting bumped by life. And then they hurt. Pain always gets my attention.

You mattered. That's why losing you is painful. I matter, though at times it doesn't feel that way. Everyone matters. We all long to be loved, don't we?

Your leaving has taught me so much. Now is the time to live. Love now. Express kindness now. Say what I need and want to say now. There may not be another opportunity.

People matter. Each one. I will remember that today.

~~~

Life is about people. We come out of the womb looking for connection and love. We naturally search for safety and unconditional acceptance. We grow and thrive when we feel seen, heard, and significant.

Most people find love by giving it. We find safety the same way. Safe, loving people tend to attract others who also value safety and close connections.

Along the way, we get hurt, and we hurt others. Our hearts are wounded. This affects the way we approach life and relationships. When someone we care about leaves or dies, our sense of safety can take a hit. We've loved, and now we've lost. This can be excruciatingly painful.

If we're willing, the loss of our spouses can teach us to live more meaningful and significant lives. Relationships take on new importance. We now know that all we have is the present moment. Nothing else is guaranteed. We set our sights on expressing our hearts, saying what we need to say and doing what we need to do.

In the end, our wounded hearts still need the same things: love and safety. We can give some of that away today. As we do, our love for others can become a salve to our own wounded hearts.

Affirmation: I will live and love today, one person, one moment at a time.

I DIDN'T KNOW WHAT
I DIDN'T KNOW

FROM THE GRIEVING HEART:

They say confession is good for the soul. I've been writing in my journal about this. Losing you has caused me to consider my own life more deeply.

Through my grief, I can look back and see mistake after mistake. Errors galore. Mainly, I see how I've judged others who were in pain. I have many regrets.

Then again, I didn't know what I didn't know. I had not experienced loss like this, so how could I understand significant emotional pain? We don't know until we've been there.

I spoke of things I didn't know anything about. I distanced myself from people who were hurting. I disappeared from some lives. I did to others the things I've been angry at others for doing to me.

Life has interesting twists. Perhaps I should contact some of these people and apologize. That might do us both good. I don't know. It's a bit scary to contemplate being that vulnerable.

For now, I will go on using my journal to express my deepest pain and the mistakes that I've made along the way. It feels good, like my soul is being cleansed.

In many cases, loss causes us to look back at our own behavior and wince. Because we had not known significant grief, many of us were less than sensitive to those in pain around us. We were uncomfortable. We didn't know what to say. As time went on, perhaps we grew impatient with them. Maybe we withdrew and distanced ourselves.

We see life differently now. We know the pain of loss and the frustration of being misunderstood. We have experienced the hurt of evaluation, judgment, and rejection at a time when our hearts were broken and bleeding. Guilt can raise its head.

Personal recognition and confession can be profoundly good and healing. As our hearts own up to what we thought, said, and did, we can better release the past and live fuller, more meaningful lives now. Confession allows us to look back, evaluate, and bring some closure to painful situations. There may even be scenarios where we can apologize or make amends.

Our hearts do better when we own up to the truth, as painful as that might be. As we do, we'll be able to engage with life and others more fully. We'll become more authentic. We'll give away more love and safety, and experience more of them in return.

Loss has many lessons for us. Since we're here, why not learn as much as we can?

> Affirmation: Losing you has taught me I can
> look back, own the hurt I've caused, and live
> more meaningfully than ever before.

FOR RELFLECTION
AND/OR JOURNALING

My Grieving Heart:
*"If someone were to ask me how
to grieve well, I would say…"*

_____

_____

_____

_____

_____

_____

_____

_____

_____

_____

_____

_____

_____

_____

_____

_____

_____

_____

_____

_____

_____

_____

_____

_____

_____

_____

_____

_____

_____

_____

_____

_____

_____

_____

WORDS ARE CRUCIAL — AND OVERRATED

FROM THE GRIEVING HEART:

Yesterday was important. I received an email from a good friend. All she said was, "I'm thinking about you."

I was amazed how that phrase affected me. I was comforted and felt loved.

So simple. "I'm thinking about you."

Words are both crucial and overrated. It seems like where there are many words, there is misunderstanding and hurt. I can be wordy, but I'm learning that the value is not in the words, but in thinking about and seeing the other person.

Losing you has taught me this. Words fix nothing. Platitudes are empty. Hearts matter. Presence counts.

"I'm thinking of you."

Nice. I need to be thought of.

I think I'll write to another grieving heart today. My message will be simple.

In grief and in life, what we say and what is said to us has great power. Words can hurt or heal. In general, however, when grief emotions are intense, the fewer the words, the better.

More important than what's said is the heart behind the words. Is the other person being thought of? Are the words more about the speaker or the recipient? Not knowing what another grieving heart might be thinking or feeling at any given moment, "I'm thinking of you," can be a wonderfully expressive statement.

It's nice to be thought of. We're being remembered with concern and affection, without evaluation, judgment, or attempts to change or fix. When grieving hearts are met where they are, even for a moment, good occurs.

Even with shattered hearts, we can do good. When we connect with other grieving souls out of genuine concern for their welfare, our own needs are partially met. We receive by giving.

We can think of each other often. We can express our affection and concern simply and authentically. The results for all of us could be extraordinary over time.

Affirmation: I can express simple kindness to
other grieving hearts. This helps all of us.

I WILL USE MY GRIEF
FOR GOOD

FROM THE GRIEVING HEART:

I talked to another grieving heart yesterday.
They said something that struck me.

"What did I ever do to deserve this?" they asked.

I blinked.

"Maybe this is my just reward for all my miscues and mistakes," they continued.

I also heard the opposite: "My loved one didn't deserve this. I don't think I deserve this either. Why is life so unfair?"

I don't know which it is. Perhaps neither. How can we as humans make judgments about such things? We don't know. We can't know.

It happened. You're gone. This is reality now. I must find ways to live on. I want to live well, remembering and honoring you along the way.

I will let go of blame. It serves no purpose. I will invest in my heart. I will never be the same, and I don't want to be. But I will heal and grow through this.

And I will use my grief for good.

***

When it comes to what happens and why, there is much we don't understand. We control little, yet we have profound influence over what and who we're connected to. The ripple effects of our lives are widespread and extraordinary.

We don't know everything — not even close. We can't be in two places at once. We have influence, but we are far less powerful than we think when we're talking about keeping bad things from happening to our spouses or other people we care about.

Our hearts might continue to question, but through the grief process, we often come to the point of accepting some of what we can't comprehend. In our own way, we have to make some sense of what happened, and then do the best we can to live on in light of it.

When we release the need to understand everything, we open our hearts up to accept this new reality. We start adjusting to our current situation. Our new normal begins to take shape.

We learn to take our souls and bodies seriously. We discover that loving ourselves is one of the greatest gifts we can give ourselves and our departed mates. We begin to jettison whatever keeps us from healing and growing.

We will never be the same, but we can still live with great significance and impact.

Affirmation: Part of grieving is learning to let go
of what is no longer helpful. I want to travel light and make a difference.

PERHAPS LETTING GO ISN'T WHAT I THOUGHT

FROM THE GRIEVING HEART:

I hear a lot about letting go. At first, this irked me.
Let go? How do I do that? I don't want to!

But perhaps letting go isn't what I thought.

On this grief journey, I've discovered that I must let go of certain
things. If I want to live, I must let the past be what it was. I
also must grieve the future I anticipated but now will never be. I
must learn to live well here without your physical presence.

I'm working to let go of guilt, shame, and blame. I want
to release the wounds and mistakes of the past and be bur-
dened by them no longer. I want to remember and honor you
while engaging in life and doing the most good I can.

Above all, I want to release my expectations. Most of the time,
they simply set me up for disappointment. I will plan yet hold
those plans loosely. All I can do is become the best version of me
possible. I choose to focus on that and take what comes.

I will practice letting go — one thing, one moment at a time.

When a grieving heart hears the phrase "letting go," our first inclina-
tion is resistance. We assume that letting go means giving up spouses or

leaving them behind. Since we're wired for connection, our instinct is to cling to them with all our might.

But what if letting go could mean something different? What if it means releasing the things that weigh us down in the grief process — things like critical influences, toxic people, unhelpful thought patterns, or self-numbing addictions? What if letting go refers to intentionally releasing what's not healthy to more fully embrace what is?

Many discover that letting go and grieving well are synonymous. As we take our hearts seriously and express our grief in healthy ways, our departed mates assume new roles in our lives. As we adjust to their absence, we begin to appreciate things about them we might have missed before. As we accept our loss, we might also be embracing them in new ways.

Grief is a truly mysterious process. It is not a program or checklist, but rather a meandering path that often doubles back on itself. Its dizzying twists and turns can be confusing, but as we continue our journey, we discover we're heading somewhere.

We don't need to know it all. We can't. But at any given moment, we can choose to release what burdens us and lean forward into what's coming.

> Affirmation: Letting go may not be what
> I thought. I can release what was and em-
> brace what is, one moment at a time.

I THINK I'M READY

FROM THE GRIEVING HEART:

I can't believe I'm about to say this. I think I'm ready.

I think I'm ready to date. I still miss you - terribly. But my grief is changing. Your loss is somehow settling into my heart. I know you're with me in many ways, and always will be. I also know you would want me to be happy and to live life.

Living life is to be in good relationships. You taught me that. I experienced it with you. I want to experience that again. I know it won't be the same - it can't be. What we had was unique and special. One of a kind.

But I believe there is still good out there for me. I believe I still have good to give to someone else. I'm tired of feeling alone, and I think I'm ready to remedy that.

My head warns me not to get carried away, to take my time, and to go slow. Yet, I know I can't exactly control all that either. My heart aches but wants to love and be loved again.

Whomever I go out with, I hope they're okay with me talking about you. Better yet, I hope they ask about you, and then listen well. You are a part of me and always will be. They need to know that and appreciate it.

I don't know how to do this. I feel awkward. Dating again? Me? Now? It's all so strange.

Most of us know when we've turned a corner in our grief and are ready to consider dating. There are some who choose to never date again, and that's okay. We're all unique and at different stages. We all have somewhat different mindsets, values, and missions. The key is being who we are, as we are, where we are - as much as possible.

For those who are contemplating dating, guilt will often surface. There is a natural wondering if we're somehow being unfaithful. In some cases, this can mean we have some unfinished business with our departed spouses that needs to be dealt with before moving forward.

Some like to have the past settled before stepping into the dating realm. Others are more apt to move ahead more quickly, trusting that what they need to work on and process will surface along the way. Again, our hearts are all unique.

If we think we're ready to date, we must acknowledge that what we had with our mate was special and one of a kind. If we're trying to replace them somehow, this will not work out well. If we know that each relationship is different and are willing to let the other person be who they are, then we're on the road to some healthy companionship.

Comparing new people in our life with our spouse is natural. In some ways, this is helpful, for we know what we want and what we don't. We know that hearts, interests, values, and convictions need to match. Knowing beforehand, however, that they are not our departed mate and never will be is helpful too.

Again, healthy movement forward is always one step at a time.

Affirmation: What we had was special and one of a kind.
I'll never find that again, because there is only one you.
But I believe there is good and love out there.

MY GRIEF IS CHANGING

FROM THE GRIEVING HEART:

My grief is changing. I can feel it.

I miss you. I always will. But the missing is somehow less intense. My heart must be adjusting to you not being here.

Ugh. I feel guilty saying that.

Life is so different now. I'm different. I used to try to control everything. Losing you has taught me just how little I can control.

Life is not what I expected. Things have not gone how I planned. I've had my share of surprises, and not all of them have been good. Pain and grief are good teachers, if I'm willing to learn from them.

I want to travel lighter. I want to live more in freedom than in fear. I want to live well without having to feel in control. This life is short, and I want to make a difference.

In some ways, you have taught me this. You continue to influence my life greatly, though you are no longer here. You are a gift to me.

Thank you.

Not many of us live free. Many go through the motions, not thinking much about life or the future. Some live unevaluated lives focused on avoiding pain and being comfortable. Many are on a treadmill they can't seem to step off.

Burdened by expectations, worries, and fears, we slog through our days. We work, strive, plot, and plan. Then death or disaster comes, and our illusions of control are dealt a shattering blow. We grieve not only the loss of our spouses, but also the death of our world as we knew it. We mourn our loss of perceived control.

As we've said before, we don't control much — perhaps only the thoughts we allow to dwell in our minds and the resulting words and actions. We have influence but not control over circumstances, other people, and life in general. In the end, we're better off accepting this reality, abandoning our futile attempts at control, and focusing on becoming the best people we can be.

Loss and grief can instruct us. We can choose to travel lighter now. We can live with greater purpose and meaning. We can practice living more in the present moment, rather than dwelling in the past or the future.

This is all a process, and most of us are slow learners. We breathe deeply. We lean forward. We try to be patient with ourselves along the way.

Affirmation: I'll keep breathing deeply, try to control
less, and practice living in the present moment.

FOR REFLECTION
AND/OR JOURNALING

My Grieving Heart:
*"As I look back, I can see my grief
changing over time. For example..."*

_____

_____

_____

_____

_____

_____

_____

_____

_____

_____

_____

_____

_____

GARY ROE

_____

_____

_____

_____

_____

_____

_____

_____

_____

_____

_____

_____

_____

_____

_____

_____

_____

_____

_____

_____

FOR REFLECTION
AND/OR JOURNALING

My Grieving Heart:
*"As I look back, I can see my grief
changing over time. For example..."*

_____

_____

_____

_____

_____

_____

_____

_____

_____

_____

_____

_____

_____

_____

_____

_____

_____

_____

_____

_____

_____

_____

_____

_____

_____

_____

_____

_____

_____

_____

_____

_____

_____

_____

I'M SMALL, BUT I MATTER

FROM THE GRIEVING HEART:

As I drove around yesterday, I found myself looking at the people in the vehicles around me. "How many of them are grieving?" I wondered.

Probably many more than I realize.

I believe that most people are hurting, worried, or fearful. After all, everyone has been wounded, and all of us have experienced loss of some kind. We just fake it. We put on a good face. We wear masks.

I pulled into a parking lot and sat there thinking. The collective pain out there stunned me. Why doesn't anyone talk about this? Why do we bury our grief and pain?

No wonder the world seems on the verge of exploding from time to time.

Inside, I felt my loss somehow take its place among all the other losses of the world. Maybe I felt a little of others' pain.

I know I've said it before, but I'll write it again. I'll put my grief to work. I am small, but I matter. I want to make a difference.

When loss strikes, most of us naturally pull inward. We're shaken and vulnerable. We're stunned and need to catch our breath. Then we begin to feel the pain and sadness. If the loss is great enough, it can begin to take over our entire existence.

When a person is in great pain, it's hard to think about anything else.

Life becomes about endurance and managing the pain as well as possible. Although this might be the stage we're in, this phase is not forever. Pain and suffering are not our new life. This is a season of loss and grief.

As we process the loss of our mates, our hearts begin to adjust and our grief changes. We still love and miss them, but the pain is different. We begin to learn to live on, with a hole in our hearts.

Our experience with loss can sensitize us to the grief and pain of those around us. Loss is everywhere. Hearts have been broken and dreams crushed. Plans have been shattered and souls shaken. We can put our grief to work and meet hurting hearts where they are. We can help bring comfort, perspective, and hope.

We're in this together. We desperately need each other. We can all make more of an impact than we realize.

Affirmation: Losing you has sensitized me to the pain of
others. Even while hurting, I can comfort others.

I'M SWIMMING UPSTREAM

FROM THE GRIEVING HEART:

I've come to a conclusion. I can either let the world and circumstances set the agenda for my life, or I can be about something bigger and better.

When I lost you, I longed for listening ears and compassionate hearts to be with me in this. Instead, what I got most of the time was impatience, judgment, and criticism. People's reactions only added to my pain rather than helping relieve it.

This isn't right. And I believe it can change. At least, I can choose to not be one of the mass of judgmental voices out there.

I choose to have a compassionate heart. I will stop and see the pain of others. I will take a moment, look in their eyes, and enter their world. I want to be a safe person that feels a tiny portion of their grief and reminds them that they are not alone.

I sense that I'm swimming upstream, but I'll bet there are others like me out there. There must be other grieving hearts who have decided to be a part of the solution to the world's pain and grief.

I will put my grief experience to work. I will pay attention, and look for opportunities.

As we move through our grief, we begin to be more aware of the struggles of others. There are wounds everywhere. Many have departed and died. Almost every heart has at least one hole in it. We're all missing someone.

Grief can produce in us new reservoirs of love and compassion. There is power and healing in reaching out to another hurting soul. We can be the soft hearts and listening ears that we ourselves longed for in our grief journey.

We have been there. We know. We understand that grieving hearts don't need fixing, judgment, or criticism. They need someone safe, someone they can call on when needed to simply be with them. We have learned that showing up and being available is a powerful offer of support and kindness.

Our hearts have been broken. Our life-web has been shaken. Our lives have been upended. Even while in pain, we can extend a hand to other grieving hearts. When two souls that know grief find each other, healing occurs.

We know the problems surrounding grief in our world. We can be a part of the solution.

Affirmation: Now that I know grief, I can
be part of the solution for other grieving hearts.
I will show up, listen, and love.

TRIGGERS ARE EVERYWHERE

FROM THE GRIEVING HEART:

Yesterday was tough. Everywhere I went, there seemed to be reminders of you. Triggers were everywhere. Grief bursts riddled the day.

I wondered what was happening. I thought perhaps I was losing it, again. I tried to collect myself, slow down, and breathe deeply. After all these months, I'm still surprised how difficult simply breathing is when grief emotions strike.

Then that old fear hit me. "What if all this grief work didn't help? What if the grief returns and takes over my life again? What if this pit is one I'll never be able to climb out of?"

I kept trying to breathe deeply and began talking to myself.

"Be kind to yourself. Be patient with yourself. This is grief. Just grieve."

In the middle of it all, I reached out to one of my safe people. Her voice was so calming. I could almost hear her smile over the phone. It was like she expected me to have another day like this at some point.

"Just breathe and grieve. This is natural and normal," she said.

Breathe and grieve.

Many naturally think that once their grief journey gets to a certain point that there will be no more bad days or emotional pain. Heart bruises can be bumped at any time, and the pain can be intense.

There is no time limit on grief bursts. We have all experienced more loss than we realize, and the grief can build up slowly over time. Suddenly it needs to be released. Grief will be expressed. This is natural, normal, and healthy.

The question is not if we will have more grief bursts, but when. When they come, we breathe through them. We can be patient with ourselves and remind our hearts that this grief is okay. Instead of fighting it, we can simply grieve.

If we're questioning our progress or our sanity, then reaching out to a safe person is an excellent option. Those who know grief can give us perspective and be extremely reassuring. Grieving hearts often need reassurance.

When these grief attacks happen to others, we can be the reassuring voice. "Just breathe and grieve. This is natural and normal."

Affirmation: I will be patient with myself and
remember that grief bursts can happen at any time,
even months or years down the road.

IT WILL BE HARD, BUT IT CAN STILL BE GOOD

FROM THE GRIEVING HEART:

Today is an important day. It's the anniversary of your leaving. I've missed you. I miss you still.

I dreaded this day, but at least I planned for it. I was tempted to stick my head in the sand and wait it out, but I knew that wouldn't be honoring to you or loving toward myself.

I remember you today. I will light a candle in your honor. I will write you a letter. I will visit one of our special places. I will breathe deeply through all of this. I will be kind to myself, patient with myself, and grieve.

I will open my heart to others and allow them to express concern for me today. I will receive gladly any gestures of kindness from friends or loved ones that may come my way. Several of my safe people know what today is. I will reach out to them at some point. It's good to have someone in this with me.

I will get out among people today and remind myself that I still live in a world of people and relationships. I will focus on seeing those around me, knowing that they too have known loss in some way.

I will make today count. It will be hard, but it can still be good.

Death anniversaries are difficult. In some cases, these days are hard for many years, perhaps even the rest of our lives. Along with the pain these times naturally bring, we can also use these days to help us grieve and to honor our life partners.

We can make a simple plan to remember them. We can do something they would enjoy. We can honor them by giving to or serving a cause that reminds us of them. We can write a letter, set up an empty chair, go to a favorite place, or engage in a special activity.

We loved them and love them still. We know them. What seems to fit best? What would help us grieve and also honor them? Can we involve others somehow?

We know this day will be hard, but it can still be good. It can be meaningful and healing. If we focus on expressing love, we can't go wrong no matter how we choose to honor them.

This anniversary is important. Every year it will stand out. We can plan for it, and make it count.

Affirmation: I will make the anniversary of your leaving count. It will be hard, but it can still be good.

ONE DAY AT A TIME

FROM THE GRIEVING HEART:

I'm looking back today. I see a lot of pain. I also see many blessings.

I remember how others treated me. Some said they would be there, then disappeared. Others avoided me and even pretended not to see me in public. Still others said unhelpful, even hurtful things.

The world didn't seem to care or even be fazed by your loss. It scurried on as if nothing happened. I was angry, frustrated, sad, and depressed. I felt guilty, stunned, and confused. I thought I was going crazy.

I discovered who was safe and who wasn't. A few came close and entered my pain. They listened. They cared. Their presence made all the difference.

I longed for your presence. Your absence permeated everything. My world changed. I changed.

I grieved. I learned. I grew. It still hurts, but I'm trying to use the pain for good.

The journey continues, one day at a time. I will live with meaning and make a difference in this hurting world. I want to positively impact the lives of those who are grieving. I'll use this giant hole in my heart to help bring hope and healing to others.

Grief alters our world. It changes everything because it changes us. No one is the same after a loss. No one.

Grief also reveals us. It unveils our hearts and shows what matters to us most deeply. Loss turns us inside out.

The loss of a spouse and the resulting grief can teach us much. We discover what's most important in life. We learn what's trivial and mere fluff. Loss can shake us into new and more positive ways of thinking, speaking, and living. None of us wants loss or pain, but once they come, there is much we can receive if we're willing.

We also begin to discern things about others that we didn't know before. We learn to recognize who's helpful and who's not. We see better what relationships are safe for us and which ones might be toxic. Clearer vision can enable wiser decision-making.

Grief is hard and painful, but it can bring many blessings. We will always miss our mates, but now we can make their lives and memory count in new ways.

Affirmation: Loss has taught me what's important and how to
live with more purpose and impact. I'm grateful for this.

I WANT TO LIVE TODAY
AS BEST I CAN

FROM THE GRIEVING HEART:

*You matter. I matter. The people around me mat-
ter. I will use my grief to love and serve.*

*I'll hurt from time to time. I have a dull ache deep inside that may
never go away. I'm okay with that. It reminds me of you. The thought of
you brings more smiles than tears these days, for which I'm thankful.*

*I could walk around afraid of death, separation, or what's going to
happen next. Or I could choose to live courageously and make each day
count. Personally, the latter seems easier and a lot more fulfilling.*

*I will live with purpose. Your departure stunned me and broke my
heart. Somehow, the shattered pieces have come together again and are
ready to live. The color is coming back into my world. My heart will
never be the same, but I believe it can be even better, because of you.*

*I will live today, as best I can. I will see others and attempt to
take a glimpse into their hearts. I want to be more understanding of their needs and their pain. I will act with kindness and
compassion. I will love, as much as I can, in each situation.*

One day, one person, one interaction, one moment at a time.

Life is full of loss. We experience it more than we realize, in more forms
than we can imagine. Most settle into a pattern of coping as best they

can with the hits that come. Some choose to attempt to dull the pain with various addictions. Others decide to take their hearts seriously, learn to grieve well, and heal.

Why do we grieve? Because we love. We connect, relate, grow close, trust, and love. When loss severs a strand of our life-web, the pain we experience is natural. Our grief proclaims our love.

Since we're meant for connection, saying goodbye is hard. In the case of a spouse, farewells are excruciating. This takes time. Most end up saying farewell in bits and pieces. Our hearts process the loss, trying to understand and find some solid ground in a suddenly shifting world.

If we embrace grief's lessons, we can end up appreciating people even more. We can live more in the present, seeing and hearing those around us. We can be aggressively kind and deeply compassionate. We can live with quiet power and purpose.

Most people feel more significant and fulfilled when they're expressing love and serving others. Perhaps doing so gets us more in touch with who we really are – unique, special individuals doing life with and for one another.

We love, and we grieve, one day, one person, one moment at a time.

Affirmation: I will make your loss count. I will love and
live life one interaction, one moment at a time.

FOR REFLECTION
AND/OR JOURNALING

My Grieving Heart:
*"When I think of using my grief
for good and to serve others, I think of...."*

_____

_____

_____

_____

_____

_____

_____

_____

_____

_____

_____

_____

_____

_____

_____

_____

_____

_____

_____

_____

_____

_____

_____

_____

_____

_____

_____

_____

_____

_____

_____

CONCLUDING THOUGHTS: A PERSONAL PERSPECTIVE ON LOSS, GRIEF, AND EMOTIONAL PAIN

"Mourn with those who mourn."

– The Apostle Paul

"In this world, you will have trouble."

– Jesus Christ

Thank you for taking your heart seriously and reading this book. I hope you found it comforting and helpful. Most of all, I trust you know you're not alone. Grief is a lonely road, but we can travel it together.

I would like to conclude by sharing my personal perspective on loss, grief, and emotional pain in the hope that somehow my experience might be beneficial to you in your journey.

I AM A FELLOW STRUGGLER

As I mentioned in the introductory chapter, I am a fellow struggler. I battle daily with issues stemming from the losses I've endured and continue to face. I stumble a lot in life.

I am a follower of Jesus Christ. I'm also inconsistent and far from perfect. I get confused, frustrated, and anxious at times. But Jesus is my life, and this influences my thoughts, actions, and how I write.

Whether you come from a different faith orientation or perhaps claim no faith at all, my goal is not to convince you of anything or cause distress of any kind. My purpose is to encourage you by sharing what has been helpful to me in navigating this up-and-down existence of grief and loss.

So please take the following for what it is: my story. Your story is your own.

MY EARLY STORY

I lost both grandfathers so early I don't remember them. Due to dementia, one grandmother never knew who I was. Though I had relatives nearby, my nuclear family was isolated and relationally distant from them. As a child, I remember feeling sad and lonely most of the time.

I lost chunks of my early childhood to repetitive, traumatic sexual abuse. This shaped my view of myself, others, the world, and God. My sadness and loneliness grew. My family experienced other close losses, and I remember the atmosphere of grief that blanketed our home. It was stifling and had a tinge of hopelessness to it.

In junior high school, a good friend died suddenly over the Christmas holidays. He sat right in front of me in homeroom. He was so bright, fun, full of promise, and healthy. I remember thinking, "How can such things happen?"

My home environment was volatile. My parents separated and divorced in my early teens. By default, I stayed with Mom. She had serious mental health issues and slipped deeper into a world of grandiose delusions. It wasn't a good situation. I moved in with Dad.

The next six months were some of the best of my life. Dad was stable, and his presence provided a strong sense of safety. Then one Sunday afternoon, he collapsed in front of me of a massive heart attack. He never regained consciousness and died a week later. My world, as I knew it, was over. I was 15.

I moved back in with Mom, who was even more unstable than before. After attempting to take her own life, she went into psychiatric care. Functionally, I was now an orphan. I wondered where the next hit was going to come from.

In my simple teenage way, I accepted reality. Life was difficult. Bad stuff was going to happen. In this world, I was going to have trouble.

Soon after this, I was taken in by my best friend's family. As I walked into their home, I felt a profound sense of safety.

Even though they already had four kids, they loved, accepted, and supported me in every way imaginable. Some days I wondered if this could be real. It was so good, in fact, that I simply couldn't take it all in.

One day, I asked the dad why he would take in a kid like me and make me a part of his family. He smiled and said, "Gary, with what Jesus Christ did for us, how could we not do this for you?"

Jesus was not new to me. I began going to church when I was 10. I was hurting and looking for hope. I got to know Jesus there. I wasn't interested in religion. I needed love and relationship.

Now, here he was again, this Jesus.

AN ADVENTURE OF HEALING

I went to college and studied Psychology. I immersed myself in service and found myself surrounded by troubled, wounded people. People like me. Ever since, my adult life has been focused on helping hurting people heal and grow. As I give, I heal a little bit more.

As I got older, the losses continued to pile up, as they do with all of us. I lost more relatives, friends, and co-workers. With each loss, the pain of past losses came visiting, adding to the grief of the present. As a missionary and pastor, I was frequently around emotional pain, grief, and loss.

Then my marriage of almost three decades ended in a divorce I did not want or agree with. The pain and confusion were intense. For the next several years, I questioned almost everything. The seemingly sudden death of my marriage was devastating. I felt my heart go numb, and then harden.

Normally positive and eager to trust others, my heart turned cautious. I walled myself off emotionally. I ignored or blocked all invitations to companionship and relationship. I was so wounded that I couldn't bring myself to risk even a conversation beyond the typical greetings and small talk.

I lived in fortress mode. Most of all, I didn't trust myself to make good decisions. I hadn't seen this coming. I felt dumb and naïve. I internally swore to myself, "I will not risk my heart again."

As I look back on my life, I can see several patterns. The biggest pattern is that when I seek God, wait, and don't try to make something happen, God surprises me. That's exactly what he did, again.

Through a truly miraculous set of coincidences, my heart warmed to an amazing lady who had lost her husband to pancreatic cancer. Her smile lit up the room. I kept pinching myself, wondering if she could actually be real. Still, I was reticent. I inched forward, slowly and cautiously. She kept smiling and chiseling away at my defenses, one wall at a time.

I used the word coincidences above facetiously. The way things came about made it clear that coincidences like this took very careful planning on the part of someone with a large and loving heart. I knew God still had a plan for me, but he had completely surprised me with how good and delightful he can be.

He turned my mourning into dancing. He took the pain and rubble of my losses and sculpted them into something that…well, I don't even have words to describe it.

When people hear I work as a hospice chaplain and grief counselor, most inevitably say, "I don't know how you do what you do." Yes, it's hard. It's heavy. I'm in the presence of death every day. Grief is part of the air I breathe. And I wouldn't trade it for anything. I get to enter people's lives at a sensitive and vulnerable time. I have the honor of walking with others through some of their darkest valleys.

Who else gets to do that?

So many are hurting. Different people with diverse backgrounds, unique relationships, deeply personal losses, and different faiths. But we all have this in common: we are human, and we experience loss.

I believe God not only knows our pain but feels it with us. We're designed for relationship. Separation is hard. Hearts break and shatter. God knows this. He walks with us, though many times we are unaware of his presence.

Then there is this Jesus character. The Bible declares him to be God who has taken on human flesh. He came among us, walked with us, and experienced the joy, delight, and love that quality relationships can bring. He also tasted the ugliness of injustice, deception, manipulation, rejection, betrayal, abuse, torture, and violent death. No one truly understood him. He knows loneliness. He is well acquainted with grief.

If he is God in human flesh, believing that he rose from the dead isn't a stretch for me. Rather, it seems plausible and natural. I believe he conquered death to offer me something better than the disappointment, pain, frustration, and loss of this world. I think he still conquers death, every day, in my life and in the lives of others.

Jesus knows. He knows grief, and he knows me. He shares my loneliness. This companion has made all the difference for me. He shows up in interesting ways. He brings the right people at the right time. His presence is constant. He reminds me this life is not all there is. Death has been conquered.

Again, this is my story. My prayer is that it brings some comfort and hope to you amid your loss and pain. We will never be the same, but we can still live with great purpose. Healing is possible.

THE HEALING ADVENTURE CONTINUES

I close with something Jesus himself said that has been profoundly comforting to me. I hope you find it so too.

> *"I have said these things to you so that in me you might*
> *have peace. In this world, you will have trouble.*
> *Take heart. I have overcome the world. So do not let*
> *your hearts be troubled, and do not be afraid."*

> – (John 16:33)

In this world, we will face trouble. Loss is part of our daily existence. Much of life is about overcoming.

Breathe deeply. Take your heart seriously. You matter.

AN INVITATION TO
MAKE A DIFFERENCE

When we serve others who are hurting, our own hearts heal a little. Over time, the comfort and caring we share with those around us can add up, bringing relief and greater health to our own wounded souls.

In the latter portion of this book, we began thinking about how to use our grief to make a difference in this world and in the lives of others. If this interests you, I would like to invite you to consider becoming a part of my Difference Maker Community. As a group, we are focused on making a positive, healing impact in the lives of those around us – especially other grieving hearts.

For more information, please contact me at contact@garyroe.com. Simply say, "I would like to know more about the Difference Maker Community," and I will respond to you personally.

Together, I believe we can make a massive difference.

Warmly,
Gary

Help us reach more grieving spouses.

Share this link -
https://www.garyroe.com/comfort-series/

Together, we can make a difference.

SUMMARY OF GRIEF AFFIRMATIONS

I'm stunned. Dazed. I must breathe…

Because my love is deep, my grief may be intense. Tears are natural and healthy.

I give myself permission to be sad. I will let the grief come.

It's okay if I get angry. I will find healthy ways to express my anger.

Loss is confusing. I'll be patient with myself.

Money and financial matters can be frustrating and draining. I'll handle them one at a time.

Life is surreal. I'm trying to make sense of things. This will take time.

There are many things I won't understand. I'll be patient with myself.

I'm missing you. Feeling alone is natural when grieving.

My heart is my most important possession. I'll take care of it today. I'll handle what I can, as I can.

I may feel numb at times. That's okay. My heart is working to manage the unmanageable.

I'll work on accepting myself while grieving, one moment, one step at a time.

All my relationships seem to be changing. I don't like this. I will hold all things loosely, forgive quickly, and grieve as best as I know how.

I feel crazy sometimes because losing you is insane. I will learn to accept that I'm not at my mental best right now.

My life is disturbed, so it makes sense my sleep would be too. I'll focus on grieving well and trust this will change over time.

I'll ride this grief roller-coaster as best I can, one moment at a time.

Though some people might disappoint me, I will grieve as best I can, given the circumstances.

Parenting feels impossible right now. I'll focus on taking care of myself and grieving in healthy ways. I'll face life one thing, one moment at a time.

When fear comes, I'll try to acknowledge it, identify it, and release it.

When anxiety strikes, I'll breathe deeply and remind myself that it will pass.

Guilt is not my friend. I must find ways to show it the door.

I will ask forgiveness and also forgive myself, so I can be free to love you and grieve well.

I will say to myself, "I forgive you." This is part of loving and honoring you.

Blaming won't bring you back. Instead, I'll forgive. I want my heart as free as possible.

Seeing other couples is hard, but it is part of my grief journey. I'll find healthy ways to express the grief that comes.

I know I need to build a new life, but I'm not ready yet. I'm too busy missing you. For now, I'll take things one step at a time, one moment at a time.

When I'm angry with God, I'll be honest about it. He can handle my emotions.

I'll grieve well by getting the time alone I need while staying connected to people who are helpful to me.

Though I'm single now, I'm still very much attached to you. When it comes to my heart, it's still we and not merely me. I'll take my time and try to not look too far ahead.

I'll try to eat well and take care of myself. You would want this.

Grief is exhausting. I'll try to have realistic expectations of myself during this time.

I will be myself and express my heart with those I trust and feel safe with. I will honor you by sharing my grief.

I'll recognize that your departure changes all our family relationships. This is stressful and confusing. I'll be patient with myself and all of us in this process.

If I discover something I didn't know that disturbs me, I will guard my heart. I will be honest with myself and try to process that information well.

I not only lost you but much of what was attached to you. I will be kind to myself because this is hard.

I can't expect others to understand my grief, but I will work to find some who will be respectful and considerate.

Grief is hitting my body too. I'll be kind to myself and take the best care of myself possible.

When unhelpful, insensitive words are said, I will protect my heart and release them as quickly as possible.

Some will try to fix me and my grief. I will remember that their words are usually more about them than about me.

I miss you and long to hear your voice. I love you.

As long as I'm grieving, I'll be careful about engaging in a new relationship. I want to take my heart seriously and honor you with how I live.

I will be proactive and make a simple plan for your birthday. I will honor you and express my love.

I will be proactive and plan for how I will handle the grief bursts that come.

I will engage in life today as best as I can, remembering you.

I will find people who will listen and walk this grief road with me.

I'll release guilt and forgive myself as many times as necessary. Grief is heavy enough.

What I believe might be shaken or undergo some intense examination. This is natural.

Even if I feel empty and apathetic, I'll be patient with myself. I trust this will change over time.

I will accept myself and trust that any depression I experience is temporary and will pass with time.

If my depression deepens, I'll reach out for help. This is part of loving myself, and you.

I'll find ways to express my grief without comparing my loss to that of others. Comparison does not help me grieve well.

Life is tough and losing you is painful. There's plenty to scream about.

It's hard to imagine a future without you in it. I will focus on grieving well and celebrating you along the way.

I can't control the words and actions of others. I'll focus on grieving and being the best me possible in this situation.

Even if others don't mention you, I will. I'll give us a chance to grieve together.

If asked for companionship, I'll respond kindly and honestly. I'll take my time. My heart is at stake.

I'm lonely, and that's okay. I miss you. I also miss companionship. I'll take my time and trust that I'll know what the next step is when it's time.

Since I now know grief, I can engage with other grieving hearts. This could be good for all involved.

Even though I'm hurting, I can comfort others. My pain has purpose.

With family, I'll open my heart to those who are supportive and limit my exposure to those who aren't.

Grieving is a process. I'll be patient with myself and accept myself along the way.

If I feel less connected to you, I won't panic. This is part of grief.

I will speak your name and tell your story. This helps me grieve and is part of loving myself and you.

When fear of more loss comes, I'll acknowledge the fear and release it. This is part of grieving and living well.

When grief bursts come, I will breathe deeply and feel them through. These times are steps forward, not backward.

Rather than dreading special days, I will make plans to remember and honor you. This is part of loving myself and you.

My heart needs to continually express itself to be healthy and to heal. I'll find a way to do this.

I will live and love today, one person, one moment at a time.

Losing you has taught me I can look back, own the hurt I've caused, and live more meaningfully than ever before.

I can express simple kindness to other grieving hearts. This helps all of us.

Part of grieving is learning to let go of what is no longer helpful. I want to travel light and make a difference.

Letting go may not be what I thought. I can release what was and embrace what is, one moment at a time.

What we had was special and one of a kind. I'll never find that again, because there is only one you. But I believe there is good and love out there.

I'll keep breathing deeply, try to control less, and practice living in the present moment.

Losing you has sensitized me to the pain of other people. Even while hurting, I can comfort others.

Now that I know grief, I can be part of the solution for other grieving hearts. I will show up, listen, and love.

I will be patient with myself and remember that grief bursts can happen at any time, even months or years down the road.

I will make the anniversary of your leaving count. It will be hard, but it can still be good.

Loss has taught me what's important and how to live with more purpose and impact. I'm grateful for this.

I will make your loss count. I will love and live life one interaction, one moment at a time.

ADDITIONAL RESOURCES

BOOKS

Difference Maker: Overcoming Adversity and Turning Pain into Purpose, Every Day

You've been hit and wounded. Life hasn't turned out to be what you expected, wanted, or hoped for. Your heart says, "There's got to be more." Yes, there is. It's time to turn things around, expose the lies you've been fed about yourself, and embrace the truth. You're a Difference Maker. And it's time to start living that way. In *Difference Maker*, you'll discover how to conquer obstacles like fear, anxiety, anger, depression, self-destructive behavior, and suicidal thoughts. You'll learn why you're here, what your mission is, and how to live with more purpose and passion than you dreamed possible. *Difference Maker* is available in adult and teen editions in various formats from most online book distributors. The world needs you. Accept the Difference Maker challenge. www.garyroe. com/difference-maker

Teen Grief: Caring for the Grieving Teenage Heart

Teens are hurting. While trying to make sense of an increasingly confusing and troubled world, teens get hit, again and again. Edgy, fun-loving, tech-driven, and seemingly indestructible, their souls are shaking. We can't afford to allow pain and loss to get the better of them. What can we do? Written at the request of parents, teachers, coaches, and school counselors, this informative, practical book is replete with guidance, insight, and ideas for assisting teens navigate the turbulent waters of loss. As they heal and grow, they can become the Difference Makers this world so desperately needs. Winner of the Book Excellence Award, *Teen*

Grief has received rave reviews from those who live and work with teens. *Teen Grief* is available in various formats from most book retailers. www. garyroe.com/teengrief

Shattered: Surviving the Loss of a Child

Unthinkable. Unbelievable. Heart-breaking. Whatever words we choose, they all fall far short of the reality. The loss of a child is a terrible thing. How do we survive this? Written at the request of grieving parents and grandparents, *Shattered* has been called "one of the most comprehensive and practical grief books available." The book combines personal stories, compassionate guidance, and practical suggestions/exercises designed to help shattered hearts navigate this devastating loss. Honored as a Best Book Awards Finalist, *Shattered* has received sterling reviews by both mental health professionals and grieving parents. It is available in various formats through most major online book retailers. www.garyroe.com/shattered

Please Be Patient, I'm Grieving: How to Care for and Support the Grieving Heart

People often feel misunderstood, judged, and even rejected during a time of loss. This makes matters more difficult for an already broken heart. It doesn't have to be this way. It's time we took the grieving heart seriously. Gary wrote this book by request to help others better understand and support grieving hearts and to help grieving hearts understand themselves. A group discussion guide is included. *Please Be Patient, I'm Grieving* was a Best Book Awards Finalist and can be found in various formats at most online bookstores. www.garyroe.com/please-be-patient

Heartbroken: Healing from the Loss of a Spouse

Losing a spouse is painful, confusing, and often traumatic. This comforting and practical book was penned from the stories of dozens of widows and widowers. It's simple, straightforward approach has emotionally impacted hearts and helped thousands know they're not alone, not crazy, and that they will make it. *Heartbroken* was a USA Best Book Award Finalist and a National Indie Excellence Book Award Finalist. Available in various formats from most major online retailers. www.garyroe.com/heartbroken-2

Surviving the Holidays Without You: Navigating Loss During Special Seasons

This warm and intensely practical volume has been dubbed a "Survival Kit for Holidays." It has helped many understand why holidays are especially hard while grieving and how to navigate them with greater confidence. Being proactive and having a plan can make all the difference. *Surviving the Holidays Without You* was a Book Excellence Award Finalist and is available in various formats from most major online retailers. www.garyroe.com/surviving-the-holidays

Saying Goodbye: Facing the Loss of a Loved One

Full of stories, this warm, easy-to-read, and beautifully illustrated gift book has comforted thousands. It reads like a conversation with a close friend giving wise counsel and hope to those facing a loss. Co-authored with New York Times' Bestseller Cecil Murphey, this attractive hardback edition is available at www.garyroe.com/saying-goodbye

FREE ON GARY'S WEBSITE

The Good Grief Mini-Course

Full of personal stories, inspirational content, and practical assignments, this 8-session email series is designed to help readers understand grief and deal with its roller-coaster emotions. Several thousand have been through this course, which is now being used in support groups as well. Available at www.garyroe.com.

The Hole in My Heart: Tackling Grief's Tough Questions

This e-book tackles some of grief's big questions: "How did this happen?" "Why?" "Am I crazy?" "Am I normal?" "Will this get any easier?" plus others. Written in the first person, it engages and comforts the heart. Available at www.garyroe.com.

I Miss You: A Holiday Survival Kit

Thousands have downloaded this brief, easy-to-read, and very personal e-book. I Miss You provides some basic, simple tools on how to use holiday and special times to grieve well and love those around you. Available at www.garyroe.com.

A REQUEST FROM THE AUTHOR

Thank you for taking your heart seriously and reading *Comfort for the Grieving Spouse's Heart*. I hope you found some comfort, healing, and practical help in its pages.

I would love to hear what you thought of the book. Would you consider taking a moment and sending me a few sentences on how *Comfort for the Grieving Spouse's Heart* impacted you?

Send me your thoughts at contact@garyroe.com.

Your comments and feedback mean a lot to me and will assist me in producing more quality resources for grieving hearts.

Thank you.

Warmly,
Gary

CARING FOR GRIEVING HEARTS

Visit Gary at www.garyroe.com and connect with him
on Facebook, Twitter, LinkedIn, and Pinterest

Links:
Facebook: https://www.facebook.com/garyroeauthor
Twitter: https://twitter.com/GaryRoeAuthor
LinkedIn: https://www.linkedin.com/in/garyroeauthor
Pinterest: https://www.pinterest.com/garyroe79/

ABOUT THE AUTHOR

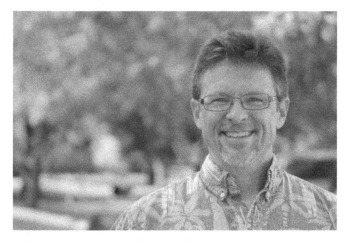

Gary's story began with a childhood of mixed messages and sexual abuse. This was followed by other losses and numerous grief experiences.

Ultimately, a painful past led Gary into a life of helping wounded people heal and grow. A former college minister, missionary in Japan, entrepreneur in Hawaii, and pastor in Texas and Washington, he now serves as a writer, speaker, chaplain, and grief counselor.

In addition to *Comfort for the Grieving Spouse's Heart*, Gary is the author of numerous books, including the award-winning bestsellers *Shattered: Surviving the Loss of a Child*, *Please Be Patient, I'm Grieving*, and *Heartbroken: Healing from the Loss of a Spouse*. He has been featured on Focus on the Family, Dr. Laura, Belief Net, the Christian Broadcasting Network, Wellness, Thrive Global, and other major media and has well over 700 grief-related articles in print. Recipient of the Diane Duncam Award for Excellence in Hospice Care, Gary is a popular keynote, conference, and seminar speaker at a wide variety of venues.

Gary loves being a husband and father. He has seven adopted children, including three daughters from Colombia. He enjoys hockey, corny jokes, good puns, and colorful Hawaiian shirts. Gary and his wife Jen and family live in Texas.

Visit Gary at www.garyroe.com.

Download your exclusive, free, printable PDF:

Healing Affirmations for Grieving Hearts
https://www.garyroe.com/healing-affirmations-for-grieving-hearts/

ABOUT THE AUTHOR

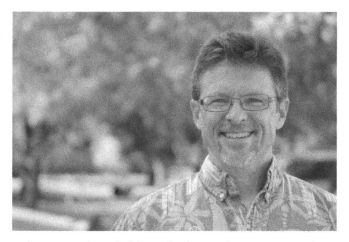

Gary's story began with a childhood of mixed messages and sexual abuse. This was followed by other losses and numerous grief experiences.

Ultimately, a painful past led Gary into a life of helping wounded people heal and grow. A former college minister, missionary in Japan, entrepreneur in Hawaii, and pastor in Texas and Washington, he now serves as a writer, speaker, chaplain, and grief counselor.

In addition to *Comfort for the Grieving Spouse's Heart*, Gary is the author of numerous books, including the award-winning bestsellers *Shattered: Surviving the Loss of a Child, Please Be Patient, I'm Grieving*, and *Heartbroken: Healing from the Loss of a Spouse*. He has been featured on Focus on the Family, Dr. Laura, Belief Net, the Christian Broadcasting Network, Wellness, Thrive Global, and other major media and has well over 700 grief-related articles in print. Recipient of the Diane Duncam Award for Excellence in Hospice Care, Gary is a popular keynote, conference, and seminar speaker at a wide variety of venues.

Gary loves being a husband and father. He has seven adopted children, including three daughters from Colombia. He enjoys hockey, corny jokes, good puns, and colorful Hawaiian shirts. Gary and his wife Jen and family live in Texas.

Visit Gary at www.garyroe.com.

Download your exclusive, free, printable PDF:

Healing Affirmations for Grieving Hearts
https://www.garyroe.com/healing-affirmations-for-grieving-hearts/

AN URGENT PLEA

HELP OTHER GRIEVING HEARTS

Dear Reader,

Others are hurting and grieving today. You can help.

How?

With a simple, heartfelt review.

Could you take a few moments and write a 1-3 sentence review of *Comfort for the Grieving Spouse's Heart* and leave it on the site you purchased the book from?

And if you want to help even more, you could leave the same review on the *Comfort for the Grieving Spouse's Heart* book page on Goodreads.

Your review counts and will help reach others who could benefit from this book.

Thanks for considering this. I read these reviews as well, and your comments and feedback assist me in producing more quality resources for grieving hearts.

Thank you!
Warmly,
Gary

CPSIA information can be obtained
at www.ICGtesting.com
Printed in the USA
BVHW071733231221
624754BV00002B/144

9 781950 382200